TEN

COMMANDMENTS

SET FREE
TO
LIVE FREE

TEN
COMMANDMENTS
SET FREE
—TO—
LIVE FREE

A 10-WEEK CURRICULUM INCLUDING DAILY DEVOTIONS,
A SMALL GROUP STUDY, AND A GROUP INDUCTIVE STUDY

EDITED BY MARK DRISCOLL

Visit Resurgence Publishing online at www.theresurgence.com.

Resurgence Publishing, Inc., the Resurgence "R," and Resurgence wordmark are registered trademarks of Resurgence.

Ten Commandments Study Guide

Cover design: Mars Hill Creative

ISBN-10: 1-938805-15-1
ISBN-13: 978-1-938805-15-8

Printed in the United States of America

19   18   17   16   15   14   13
7   6   5   4   3   2   1

CONTENTS

INTRODUCTION:
SET FREE TO LIVE FREE

FOUR HUNDRED YEARS is a long time. That's how long God's people lived away from their home, suffering bondage at the hand of the Egyptians. At long last, the Lord delivers the children of Israel from physical slavery—and they promptly fall into spiritual slavery, worshiping false gods instead of the true God.

In a great demonstration of patience, love, and grace, the Lord responds by providing instruction and wisdom for his people. He gives them the law, summarized in the Ten Commandments, to help them understand that God is the one who liberates them, not only from the shackles of Pharaoh but ultimately from slavery to sin.

New Era, Same Old Story

Like ancient Israel, God's people today often receive the gift of salvation but remain enslaved to sin. We find ourselves following in the same patterns of depression, jealousy, lust, anger, or fear. Thankfully, through his word, God reminds us that Jesus is our greater Moses who delivers a larger nation to a greater freedom. According to the Bible, our biggest problem—the problem underlying all of our other problems—is worshiping the wrong things:

> You shall have no other gods before me. You shall not make for yourself a carved image, or any likeness of anything that is in heaven above, or that is in the earth beneath, or that is in the water under the earth. You shall not bow down to them or serve them (Exod. 20:3–5).

These are the first two of the Ten Commandments. Actually, the Old Testament records over 600 commandments, often reduced to the Ten. But everything hinges on the first two: "You shall have no other gods before me" and "You shall not make idols." Many people—including hundreds of years of Jewish tradition—approach God's law as a moral checklist.

The truth is, our behavior is merely the result of who or what we worship. Our god influences our priorities, our values, our morality, our choices, and ultimately our eternity. Everyone worships something, be it money, self, comfort, sex, a significant other, children, sports, or whatever. These false gods will not only disappoint, they will imprison us to a life of addiction, greed, jealousy, insecurity, and other effects of sin. Only the one true God can break the cycle and set us free.

All of the commandments that follow the first two are simply applications of God's overarching call to "have no other gods before me." We cannot steal, murder, commit adultery, or lie if we're loving God and worshiping him. In counseling, in small group, in church, or in conversation, we can address an infinite number of moral issues, or we can boil it down to this: there's one God—worship him.

Our Gracious, Loving Father

There's a common notion that the God of the Old Testament and the God of the New Testament are two different deities, as if Old Testament God is angry and vindictive while New Testament God is gracious and loving. Throughout Scripture, however, we see that "I the LORD do not change" (Mal. 3:6), and in God's character "there is no variation or shadow due to change" (Jas. 1:17). This is absolutely evident in the story of the Ten Commandments.

God prefaces the Ten Commandments by saying, "I am the LORD your God, who brought you out of the land of Egypt, out of the house of slavery" (Exod. 20:2). This sentiment echoes throughout the New Testament for God's people today. To paraphrase Galatians 5:1, "I just set you free, so now live free." The big idea has never changed: the pathway to true freedom has less to do with physical liberation and everything to do with the object of our worship.

God's people in the Old Testament and God's people in the New Testament can enjoy a worshipful relationship with their Father, thanks to his grace and mercy—not our merit, works, or law-keeping. The Ten Commandments are not a formula for clean living; they're a picture of what it looks like to live in freedom under the protection, wisdom, and goodness of a Father who loves us.

Whether you choose to focus on the Daily Devotions, the Small Group Study, the Group Inductive Study, or all three parts of this book, I pray that your relationship with your Father grows as you learn what it means to truly live free.

—*Pastor Mark Driscoll*

COMPONENTS OF THIS STUDY GUIDE

This study guide is the result of a collaborative effort between Pastor Mark Driscoll and Mars Hill Church staff, Docent Research Group, and faithful volunteers. This ten-week study comprises three parts:

1. Daily Devotions
2. Small Group Study
3. Group Inductive Study

The **Daily Devotions** were written to facilitate dinnertime conversation with your family. These reflections are geared toward a younger audience but are written in a way that will be challenging to all. Five devotions are provided for each week's Scripture passage, and you're encouraged to use these in whatever way best fits the weekly rhythms of your family.

The **Small Group Study** is intended for small group Bible studies. Many churches encourage these types of midweek studies, and each shares the same goal—that the people of God gather together in community to study the word, encourage one another, pray, and get equipped for the mission of making the gospel of Jesus known to each group member, their families, and communities.

The **Group Inductive Study** encourages digging deep into Scripture and employs an in-depth reading technique set in a discussion-based setting. An inductive study asks the questions, "What does the Bible say, and what does it mean?" "What do we observe, and how should we interpret it in light of the whole truth of the Bible?" This portion of the study guide focuses on delving deep into the text in a collaborative environment and is a great complement to the Daily Devotions and Small Group Study material.

For additional resources on how to use these studies, please refer to the Appendix for Leaders.

THE TEN COMMANDMENTS

    I. You shall have no other gods before me.

   II. You shall not make idols.

  III. You shall not take the name of the LORD your God in vain.

  IV. Remember the Sabbath day, to keep it holy.

   V. Honor your father and your mother.

  VI. You shall not murder.

 VII. You shall not commit adultery.

VIII. You shall not steal.

  IX. You shall not bear false witness against your neighbor.

   X. You shall not covet your neighbor's house, your neighbor's wife, or anything that is his.

DAILY
DEVOTIONS

WEEK 1

You shall have no other gods before me

DAY 1

Q: What is the first commandment?

A: *You shall have no other gods before me.*

What does this mean?

We should worship, love, and trust in God more than anything else.

What do you love? What do you *really* love? If someone asked you that question, what would you say? The Bible says that we were made to worship but that our worship should be directed toward God alone. Nothing else in all creation should be seen as the most important thing in the world. God alone is. That doesn't mean that other things are not important. It just means that God alone is the *most* important.

Read *Exodus 20:2–3.*

- Do you notice anything different between verses 2 and 3? Take a look and see if you can find what it is. Both verses contain the word "god," but the word appears differently. Did you notice that? Why do you think that is?
- In the English language, we use a capital letter to signify importance. In this case, the true God gets a capital *g* and the false gods get a lowercase *g*. This is our way of denoting that anything else that we worship besides God is false. There is nothing greater than our God. That's why God commands us to worship him.

Prayer

Dear God, please help us ascribe to you the worth, value, and honor that you are due. We are tempted to worship other things but want to worship you alone. Help us in our unbelief. Forgive us our sin and give us eyes to see the true nature of your beauty, majesty, and glory. In Jesus' name we pray. Amen.

DAILY DEVOTIONS

DAY 2

Q: What is the first commandment?
A: You shall have no other gods before me.

What does this mean?
We should worship, love, and trust in God more than anything else.

What would you think if one of your friends said, "I want you to worship me!"? Would that be right? Of course not! Why would that be wrong?

Your friends are probably pretty cool, but they're certainly not God. And if they asked you to worship them, wouldn't you think they were being a bit self-centered and arrogant? Why then is it OK for God to ask us to worship him and him alone? Doesn't that make him self-centered and arrogant, too?

The reason why it would be wrong of your friends to ask you to worship them is simple: they're not God. We shouldn't worship that which isn't God. But if God is God, wouldn't it be unloving of him to not command us to love him, knowing that he himself is the greatest thing in all the universe?

God loves us and wants to give us the best. Don't you want access to the greatest thing in the universe? God knows that we do, so in love he gives us himself and calls us to worship him alone.

Read *Psalm 97:7.*

- What happens to those who worship false gods (i.e., images)?
- Does that sound very happy? What does it mean to be "put to shame"?
- In what ways are you tempted to boast or brag about things that are not God—maybe your house, school, sports teams, friends, money, music accomplishments, or clothes?

Prayer
Father, you are so good to give us yourself. Thank you for showing us that we can experience true joy by worshiping you and you alone. May we never turn to idols. Protect us from the enemy who would like to steer us away from you. Help us keep our eyes fixed on you. Amen.

DAY 3

Q: What is the first commandment?

A: You shall have no other gods before me.

What does this mean?

We should worship, love, and trust in God more than anything else.

Do you know where the word "worship" comes from? It literally means to ascribe worth to something. It's very close to the word "worth." Make sense?

Why are we tempted to ascribe ultimate worth to, or worship, things that are not God? One reason may be because these things are experienced in everyday life. Another is, these things are good. So, we often see, touch, taste, and hear lots of really cool things in God's creation. But just because something is readily accessible and good doesn't mean that they can be a suitable replacement for God. Good things that God has made can turn into really bad things.

It's hard to remember this sometimes, isn't it? All this good stuff is so engrained in our lives. But God has made them good, so that he would be the one worshiped.

Read *2 Corinthians 4:16–18.*

- Why does Paul, the author of this letter to the church in Corinth, encourage us to focus on things that are unseen? *(Because that which is unseen is eternal.)*
- What are some "seen" things that you are tempted to worship instead of God?
- What should we do when we realize we might be worshiping something other than God?

Prayer

Father, thank you for giving us so many amazing gifts. Help us to remember that all the gifts that you have given us are not you and should never replace you. Help us to love you, the giver of these gifts, more than the gifts themselves. In Jesus' name we pray. Amen.

DAILY DEVOTIONS

DAY 4

Q: What is the first commandment?
A: You shall have no other gods before me.

What does this mean?
We should worship, love, and trust in God more than anything else.

The word "and" can be dangerous. If you are eating birthday cake and the person who made it tells you that it's birthday cake "and" just a little bit of poison was added as well, that creates a huge problem for those who are eating it!

Consider the following phrases: "I love to take tests at school 'and' cheat just a little bit." "I like to drive cars 'and' drink alcohol while I drive." "I love to read books 'and' talk at the same time." Don't these statements sound ridiculous, unsafe, and counterproductive? Certain things should never be mixed—like test taking and cheating, drinking and driving, and reading and talking. Make sense?

God wants to communicate the same thing about our worship. We can't say that we love God and love false gods at the same time. They are mutually exclusive; one cancels out the other. God knows that worshiping him alone is freedom, and his commandments are meant to set us free from sin and worship of false gods.

Read *Matthew 6:24.*

- How does this verse relate to what was just read?
- How does this verse relate to the first commandment?
- Why is it easy to worship money?
- Why does money make a really bad god?

Prayer
Father, may we love and serve you alone. Teach us what a blessing it is to do this. May we banish idols from our view and fix our eyes on you. Help us when we fail. We need your help because we live in a sin-sick world with false gods all around us. Apart from you, we can do nothing. Hold us close. In Jesus' name we pray. Amen.

DAY 5

Q: What is the first commandment?

A: You shall have no other gods before me.

What does this mean?

We should worship, love, and trust in God more than anything else.

Who gets to go first? When there is a birthday party, the birthday boy or girl gets to have the first and biggest piece of cake. When there are guests over for dinner, it's best to serve them first. When someone gets first place in a competition, a trophy awaits them.

Being first is often the place of highest honor, isn't it? When someone is first, it means that there is no one ahead of them. Said differently, there is no one "before" them.

That is what God is trying to communicate here. He is saying that he should be first in our lives. There should be no one or no thing "before" him. That's because God is first. He's the best. God is God.

Anything else we place first will ultimately fail us. God is the only person in the universe who can deliver on his promises every time and won't let us down when we make him first.

Read *Psalm 96:1–6.*

- According to this text, why should we not worship idols?
- In contrast to the worship of idols, what are some ways this text suggests we worship God?

Prayer

Father, may you help us to make you first in our lives. Thank you that you love us enough to warn us about the pitfalls of worshiping false gods. We want to worship you and you alone because we know that true life and satisfaction is found only in you. May you bring help and healing to our idolatrous hearts. In Jesus' name we pray. Amen.

WEEK 2

You shall not make idols

DAY 1

Q: What is the second commandment?

A: You shall not make idols.

What does this mean?

Because we love and worship God, we should not make our own pretend gods.

Consider this passage from Isaiah 44:13–17:

> *13* The carpenter stretches a line; he marks it out with a pencil. He shapes it with planes and marks it with a compass. He shapes it into the figure of a man, with the beauty of a man, to dwell in a house. *14* He cuts down cedars, or he chooses a cypress tree or an oak and lets it grow strong among the trees of the forest. He plants a cedar and the rain nourishes it. *15* Then it becomes fuel for a man. He takes a part of it and warms himself; he kindles a fire and bakes bread. Also he makes a god and worships it; he makes it an idol and falls down before it. *16* Half of it he burns in the fire. Over the half he eats meat; he roasts it and is satisfied. Also he warms himself and says, "Aha, I am warm, I have seen the fire!" *17* And the rest of it he makes into a god, his idol, and falls down to it and worships it. He prays to it and says, "Deliver me, for you are my god!"

Reflection

- What do you think is the prophet Isaiah's main point that he wants to convey to his people?
- We might think Isaiah's audience was quite foolish to bow down to what they made with their own hands, but are there things in your life that are created by the hands of people that you are tempted to worship (e.g., technology, music, clothes, friends, grades, etc.)?
- How does this passage of Scripture help you understand the second commandment better?

DAILY DEVOTIONS

Prayer

Father, thank you so much that your word shows us how stupid it is to worship things we've made with our own hands. Give us enough wisdom to worship you, the maker of *our* hands, minds, hearts, and the giver of our every breath. Apart from you we can do nothing. In Jesus' name we pray. Amen.

DAY 2

Q: *What is the second commandment?*

A: *You shall not make idols.*

What does this mean?

Because we love and worship God, we should not make our own pretend gods.

A long time ago, God's people, called the people of Israel, were enslaved to an evil ruler. After many difficult years, God appointed a man named Moses to lead Israel out from under Pharaoh's cruel reign. Moses led Israel to a home, which God had promised to give—a place where they could live freely. God gave them a set of "family rules" called the Ten Commandments—instructions that would show them how to live well in this newfound freedom.

As Moses was on Mount Sinai receiving the Ten Commandments, the people started getting anxious, wondering what was taking him so long. They soon ran out of patience and decided that they didn't need Moses or even God: they would follow their own rules and make their own god, one they could see with their own eyes. They asked Aaron, Moses' brother and right hand man, to make for them a golden calf that they could bow down to and worship.

Read *Exodus 32:1–6.*

- Why was this such a horrible thing to do? *(God had just rescued them from Pharaoh. They saw the miracles God had done with their own eyes.)*
- Why do you think they did this? *(Impatience, lack of faith, wanting what the other nations had, etc.)*
- What do you think God did in response to this? *(You may want to read the rest of the account in Exod. 32.)*

WEEK 2

Prayer

Father, may you become so important in our lives that the thought of making something with our own hands and worshiping it would be utterly detestable. May Jesus' cross and resurrection define our lives. May you guide our worship and give us faith for the present and future. Help us work through our impatience. At times we are like the Israelites, losing faith in you. Help us. Forgive us when we fail. We know you do because of Jesus. In his name we pray. Amen.

DAY 3

Q: *What is the second commandment?*

A: You shall not make idols.

What does this mean?

Because we love and worship God, we should not make our own pretend gods.

Do you know what a genie in a bottle is? If so, do you know how it works? If not, this is the gist of it: A magical genie supposedly lives in a bottle, and if you find this bottle, you can rub it and the genie will come out. When it does, you'll be granted a wish, because the genie has the power to give you whatever you wish for. Kind of cool, right?

Part of the reason why God doesn't want us to make images of him is that we might be tempted to use those images like a genie in a bottle. If we were to make a statue of God and carry it around with us to remind us that God is with us, we might be tempted to think that God somehow lives inside that statue and that we can control him.

But that's not right: God is not supposed to grant our wishes. He is not obligated to do anything he doesn't want to do. We are obligated to follow him alone. God is not like a genie in a bottle, and we can't assume that he is.

Read *Acts 17:24–25.*

- Who is it that provides all that you need?
- What does this text tell you about God?
- What does this text tell you about the kind of people we are?
- Does God have needs?

Prayer

Father, thank you that you promise to provide for our needs and that you have no weaknesses in you that can be filled by us. We gladly submit to your rule and reign. Forgive us when we fail. We know that you do because of Jesus. In his name we pray. Amen.

DAY 4

Q: What is the second commandment?

A: You shall not make idols.

What does this mean?

Because we love and worship God, we should not make our own pretend gods.

Do you know what the word "majesty" means? Majesty means that something is impressive, beautiful, or stately. We would say that stunning mountain ranges like the Rocky Mountains or the Swiss Alps are "majestic" in their beauty.

What would you think of a friend who piled up a bunch of dirt in their backyard and then declared to you and everyone else that they had just created the Rocky Mountains? Sounds rather silly, doesn't it? It's almost insulting to the beauty of those mountains, isn't it? Those Rocky Mountains wouldn't be that impressive if one could simply create a pile of dirt and call it the Rocky Mountains.

This is another reason why God doesn't want us to make images of him: we could never represent God in a way that did justice to his impressiveness, beauty, and stateliness; all of the things that we could make with our hands would be nothing but a pile of dirt compared to him.

Read Isaiah 43:10–11.

- Was there anything before God?
- Is there anything "besides" God that can save? *(God has no equal, especially something we craft with our hands. Nothing can stand next to him as an equal.)*

Prayer

Father, help us to realize that nothing we could ever make with our hands could compare to who you really are. Give us eyes of faith to see what we can't. We trust your word and your revelation of yourself in Jesus. Thank you that you're able to keep us from following idols. In Jesus' name we pray. Amen.

DAY 5

Q: What is the second commandment?

A: You shall not make idols.

What does this mean?

Because we love and worship God, we should not make our own pretend gods.

Israel was a nation of people who were set apart for God and called to display to the world what it looked like to have God as their King. God loved them so much that he made a "covenant" with them. Do you know what a covenant is?

A covenant is a relationship between two parties that is based on love. Both parties in the covenant agree to do certain things for each other out of love. It's very similar to a marriage relationship: when a man and a woman love each other, they make a covenant to love and serve each other for life. God made a similar arrangement with Israel.

One of the reasons why God commanded Israel to not make idols was that it went against his covenant. While the nations around them all had idols, worshiping what their own hands had made, Israel was called to worship the living God alone by keeping the covenant.

Read *Exodus 34:10.*

- Could the idols of other nations do what God could do? Why or why not?
- Who holds the power in our covenant relationship with God?
- Are you trusting in him alone and not idols? How could this trust be displayed?

Prayer

Father, please make your power and glory known through us just like you did for Israel long ago. Thank you that we have a special relationship with you because of Jesus. Thank you that we don't have to go to created things to satisfy us: we can go to you, the one true and living God. In Jesus' name we pray. Amen.

WEEK 3

You shall not take the name of the LORD your God in vain

DAY 1

Q: *What is the third commandment?*

A: *You shall not take the name of the LORD your God in vain.*

What does this mean?

Because we love and worship God, we should not use his name to curse, swear, lie, or cheat. Instead, we should call his name whenever there's trouble, whenever we pray, and whenever we praise and thank him.

What does your name represent? Do you know if it has a special meaning?

For many of us in our culture today, our name is simply a name. It doesn't hold any special significance other than the reference it provides. But this was not the case with names in the Bible. And it is especially not the case with names referring to God. There are many names for God in the Bible, and they all point to some aspect of his character and nature.

"El Shaddai" means "God almighty." He is all-powerful. "Adonai" means "Lord." He is the ruler. The name "Jesus" means "Savior" because he saves us by his death and resurrection. But the most frequent name for God is the name "Yahweh." This one is a bit harder to understand, but it most likely suggests that he is real, present, and accessible to all those who call on him for deliverance or forgiveness.

The point is that the names of God represent who he *is*.

So, if there is any word that is not to be used flippantly or carelessly, it's God's name. That is why we don't say "God" or "Jesus Christ" unless we are seeking to honor and speak well of him. Sadly, most people in our culture don't share this belief and use God's name in a way that dishonors him, even as a curse word.

God's name is holy.

Read *Exodus 34:6.*

- What does this verse tell you about God's character?
- Of those attributes of God listed, which one are you most thankful for?

DAILY DEVOTIONS

Prayer

Father, thank you for reminding us who we're referring to when we say your name. May we honor you when we talk about you. Help us to view your name as something that is precious and holy. In Jesus' name we pray. Amen.

DAY 2

Q: *What is the third commandment?*

A: *You shall not take the name of the* LORD *your God in vain.*

What does this mean?

Because we love and worship God, we should not use his name to curse, swear, lie, or cheat. Instead, we should call his name whenever there's trouble, whenever we pray, and whenever we praise and thank him.

Do you know why Christians end their prayers with the phrase "in Jesus' name"? What is it about Jesus' name that makes it a good wrap-up for all of our prayers? When you come to someone in the name of someone else, what does that mean?

You could walk next door to your neighbor's house and ask for a cup of sugar by saying, "Hey there! *My mom* asked me to come over here *for her* and see if you could give us a cup of sugar." You are represented by her name. Her name goes with you. The relationship that your mom has with her neighbor is transferred to you, and you're able to get the cup of sugar because of your mom. If you didn't come as a representative of your mom, your neighbor might wonder why you needed the sugar.

It works that way when we pray. We have no authority to ask God anything on our own. But because Jesus is our representative, we can come to the Father boldly and ask for whatever we need. When we pray "in Jesus' name," what we're saying is that Jesus is our representative. Because of what he achieved for us in his life, death, and resurrection, we can have confidence to ask our Father for whatever we need. That's what we're saying when we pray in his name.

Read *Hebrews 4:14–16.*

- What is a priest? *(A mediator between God and people.)*
- According to these verses, why can we have confidence when we go to God?
- What kind of throne does God have? *(A throne of grace.)* Does that give more confidence? Why?

Prayer

Father, thank you that you have saved us through Jesus. It is in his name that we come to you and you answer. Thank you so much for the privilege of prayer and the access made possible by Jesus. We are in awe that we are united to him and that all that is his becomes ours by faith. In Jesus' name we pray. Amen.

DAY 3

Q: What is the third commandment?

A: You shall not take the name of the LORD your God in vain.

What does this mean?

Because we love and worship God, we should not use his name to curse, swear, lie, or cheat. Instead, we should call his name whenever there's trouble, whenever we pray, and whenever we praise and thank him.

Since God's name represents the greatness and glory of who he is, it is right for us to view his name with a healthy degree of reverence. Do you know what "reverence" means? It means deep respect for someone or something. In light of who God is, we should show deep respect for his name.

The Bible gives us some reasons why we should show reverence for his name, and oftentimes those reasons focus on God's acts of power. Consider these verses from the book of Psalms:

Psalm 8:1 says, "O Lord, our Lord, how majestic is your name in all the earth! You have set your glory above the heavens."

Psalm 66:1–3 says, "Shout for joy to God, all the earth; sing the glory of *his name;* give to him glorious praise! Say to God, 'How awesome are your deeds! So great is your power that your enemies come cringing to you.'"

Psalm 75:1 says, "We give thanks to you, O God; we give thanks, for your name is near. We recount your wondrous deeds."

Do you see a common theme in these verses? The psalmist connects the name of God with his mighty deeds, the evidence of his glory that we can see. We should show deep reverence for the name of God because it represents all that he is and can do. And God is limitless in what he is and can do!

We should never misuse his name because of this.

Prayer

Father, thank you that you have revealed your greatness in ways we can see. Your creation is matchless in beauty. Our bodies that you have created are wondrous beyond description. Thank you for being our Creator, Savior, and Sustainer. In light of these marvelous truths, we want to honor your name with reverence and praise. Help us when we falter. In Jesus' name we pray. Amen.

DAY 4

Q: *What is the third commandment?*

A: You shall not take the name of the LORD your God in vain.

What does this mean?

Because we love and worship God, we should not use his name to curse, swear, lie, or cheat. Instead, we should call his name whenever there's trouble, whenever we pray, and whenever we praise and thank him.

How would you feel if someone used your last name as a swear word? Probably wouldn't make you feel very good, would it? That's your family's name! It's very dear to you!

Our name is a symbol of who we are. It is precious to us. One of the reasons why the name of God is precious to us is because, in a way, it is ours as well. Just like a woman receives a new last name and identity when she marries a man, we too receive a new name and identity when we enter into a covenant relationship with God.

When someone is baptized soon after becoming a Christian, we hear these words: "I baptize you *in the name of* the Father, the Son, and the Holy Spirit." The name of God is now our name. We are his and he is ours. That's why the name of God is precious to us and shouldn't be used in a way that does not honor it.

Read *Matthew 28:19, 20.*

- When we make disciples, whose family do they become apart of?
- Based on this text, who is invited to receive God's family name?

Prayer

Father, thank you that you have given us a new name. We find our security in you and the fact that you have adopted us into your family. May you continue to remind us of our new name and identity. Draw others to our family from every tribe, tongue, and nation. Use us! May our family continue to expand, and may we feel the joy of our name being spread to others. In Jesus' name we pray. Amen.

DAY 5

Q: What is the third commandment?

A: You shall not take the name of the LORD your God in vain.

What does this mean?

Because we love and worship God, we should not use his name to curse, swear, lie, or cheat. Instead, we should call his name whenever there's trouble, whenever we pray, and whenever we praise and thank him.

Do you feel good knowing that your parents hear you when you call their name? Maybe you once had a nightmare and called out to Mom or Dad in the night, and they came to comfort you. That's great, isn't it? You know their name, and they respond when you call.

The same is true in our relationship with God. He hears us when we call. We know his name: "Father." "Jesus." "Spirit." "Yahweh." "Jehovah." "Lamb of God." "Mighty God." "King of Kings." The list goes on and on. The point is that God has revealed himself to us, and he loves it when we call on him.

Another reason why we don't use God's name flippantly or disrespectfully is because knowing his name is a privilege. Not everyone on this earth knows the name of God. And those who don't know it can't call on him. But we have a great blessing: we do know it and can call on him—anytime.

So, we have to give others the opportunity to know his name, too. God wants to be known and called upon by all.

Read *Psalm 116:1, 2.*

- Why does the psalmist say he loves the Lord?
- Based on this text, how long are we supposed to call on God?
- In what ways do you need God to hear you in the upcoming days and weeks?

Prayer

Father, your name has been revealed to us so that we can know you. We are very grateful to know you. Thank you also for helping us when we call on you. May we always call on you and never believe that we can do anything on our own. You promise to hear us, be with us, and never forsake us. We thank you so much for giving us your name. In Jesus' name we pray. Amen.

WEEK 4

Remember the Sabbath day, to keep it holy

DAY 1

Q: *What is the fourth commandment?*

A: *Remember the Sabbath day, to keep it holy.*

What does this mean?

Because we love and worship God, we should love and respect the preaching of his word, and gladly listen and learn from it.

God desires that we take a break sometimes. He knows this is really good for us. One of the reasons why it is good is that it reminds us that *we are not God*. And that is a very good thing.

Sometimes we think our lives are all about us. We believe that we are our own provider through the money we earn or the relationships we make. But God wants us to know that he is our provider. He is the one who gives us all that we need and that without him we could do nothing.

So when we rest from working, we are making a statement: "God, I recognize that I can be at rest at least one day a week because you are my ultimate provider. You hold the world together, not me. You don't need me, but I sure do need you."

Read *Philippians 4:19.*

- Who is the ultimate giver in our lives?
- What are some of the most important needs of life?
- Is there anything that God cannot provide for you?

Prayer

Father, thank you that you sustain all things by your power and that we can trust in your power to give us all that we need. May our lives display that we understand this. Help our unbelief that leads us to want to control everything. You are in ultimate control, and we acknowledge that. Thank you for rest. May we enjoy you in it. In Jesus' name we pray. Amen.

DAY 2

Q: What is the fourth commandment?

A: Remember the Sabbath day, to keep it holy.

What does this mean?

Because we love and worship God, we should love and respect the preaching of his word, and gladly listen and learn from it.

Do you like to sleep? Maybe you're younger and don't like bedtime. Maybe you are a teenager, and sleep, or sleeping in, is one of your favorite pastimes. Whether you like to go to bed or not, sleep is an essential part of being human.

Did you know that if you deprived yourself of sleep, after a few days you would start hallucinating (i.e., dreaming while awake)? Sleep reminds us that we are weak and needy. We have to sleep! We can't live without it. If we tried, we would cease to function properly. Rest is vital to our health.

We observe Sabbath for many reasons. Sometimes we just need to stop working and remind our spirit that God is in control. But God also gives us Sabbath so that we would rest our bodies and minds. He is the creator of all, and he knows that our bodies need rest in order to be healthy and happy.

Read *Psalm 121.*

- Does God ever sleep?
- How should that relate to our sleeping? *(We can rest in peace because God is in control and will keep our life.)*

Prayer

Father, thank you that you never sleep or slumber. Thank you that we can trust in you and that we can cease our working, knowing that you are our true provider. May we rest well because we know you love us. In Jesus' name we pray. Amen.

DAY 3

Q: What is the fourth commandment?

A: Remember the Sabbath day, to keep it holy.

What does this mean?

Because we love and worship God, we should love and respect the preaching of his word, and gladly listen and learn from it.

Do you know what the word "holy" means?

The word "holy" means to set something apart. To make it special. To make it different. To make it unordinary.

That is how God wants us to treat the day of worship. It should be different from the other days of the week. We should rest, but we should also focus on God and his word.

So, if at all possible, we shouldn't skip church, because church is one of the ways that we grow as a disciple. And without it, we would be weak spiritually. This is because the Spirit shapes us through the hearing of God's word. In addition, when we sing to God together, it helps us unite with other believers. And when we gather, we get to relate to one another in loving relationship, which God has created us for.

For these reasons, it is wise for us to set apart the day of worship in our minds and hearts as holy to the Lord.

Read *2 Timothy 3:16, 17.*

- How do these verses describe the importance of listening to the preaching of God's word?
- What are some of the benefits of knowing God's word?

Prayer

Father, thank you for giving us the words of life in the Bible. Thank you that you have shown us the importance of regularly listening to it being preached. May we make Sundays holy to you. May you use it to grow us into disciples who love you with all our heart, soul, mind, and strength. In Jesus' name we pray. Amen.

DAY 4

Q: What is the fourth commandment?

A: Remember the Sabbath day, to keep it holy.

What does this mean?

Because we love and worship God, we should love and respect the preaching of his word, and gladly listen and learn from it.

When this command was given to the people of Israel while enslaved in Egypt, they were used to working all day long, seven days a week. Slaves didn't get a break. They also didn't have the freedom to worship God either. So, the Sabbath command came as a blessing: they were free to work, worship, and rest.

For us, this means we need to "shut off" our mental fixation with work and technology, and focus on the fact that God sustains us. Since Jesus did the ultimate work that we could never do for ourselves, we are free to rest in him. So feel free to turn off the iPhone and take a nap. It will be good for you.

Read *Matthew 11:28–29.*

- Why does God care about our resting?
- Where is true rest found?
- Are there ways that you need to do a better job of truly resting in Jesus?

Prayer

Father, help us to rest in you. Help us to focus our minds off our work and place our hope, trust, and life in you through meditation on your word. Thank you that you tell us to come to you for rest. We need it. May we find our greatest rest in the peace you bring us through your life, death, and resurrection. In Jesus' name we pray. Amen.

DAY 5

Q: What is the fourth commandment?

A: Remember the Sabbath day, to keep it holy.

What does this mean?

Because we love and worship God, we should love and respect the preaching of his word, and gladly listen and learn from it.

What's something you look forward to? Birthdays? Concerts? The last day of school?

The Sabbath is important because it looks forward to something. Do you know what that is? While it is a day to rest from work and remember God and his work for us, it's also a symbol: there is coming a day when we will finally enter into a completely restful state that will never end. We will completely rest from our sin, suffering, and sorrow.

Just like the Lord's Supper points forward to a future day when we will sit down and eat in celebration at the marriage supper of the Lamb, our weekly Sabbath reminds us that there is coming a day when we will finally rest in Jesus for all eternity, and the turmoil of our current existence will be over for good. Isn't that good news?!

Read *Revelation 21:1–5.*

- What sounds most attractive to you about this description of the future? Does it sound restful to you?
- How can we be sure that we will get to participate in this rest?

Prayer

Father, thank you that you have given us a picture of our future rest in you. We long for it, and we thank you that it has been promised to all those who love and follow you. May our weekly rest remind us of this truth. And may we be bold to invite others to join us in the eternal rest that you will one day provide. In Jesus' name we pray. Amen.

WEEK 5

Honor your father and your mother

DAY 1

Q: What is the fifth commandment?

A: Honor your father and your mother.

What does this mean?

Because we love and worship God, we shouldn't ignore or anger our parents, but we should love, honor, obey, and think highly of them.

Do you know what it means to "honor" someone? It means to highly respect, or esteem, her. It means that you think highly of him and speak well of him. It means that you listen to her well and respond to her requests.

Why do you think God would want children to act this way toward their parents? One of the reasons is that when you honor your parents, it shows your love for God. If you don't love, listen to, and obey God, it would also be easy not to love, listen to, or obey your parents. God views your relationship with your parents as a reflection of your relationship with him. As your parents want what is best for us, so does God. So, listen to him. Honor your father and your mother.

To be sure, your parents are not God, but they love you the best they can and should repent when they fail. They need Jesus just like you do. But it is important to remember that they have been placed over you to be a good, loving, and right representative of God. When you honor them, you honor God.

Read *Ephesians 6:1.*

- What are some ways that you could honor your parents in the next few days?
- How do your parents do a good job leading, loving, and guiding you?
- Why do you think God wants you to honor your parents?

Prayer

Father, thank you that you give us parents who love us and provide for us. Help us to honor you in the way that we relate to them. May we see their authority as a reflection of yours. May submissive listening and learning characterize our response to them. Thank you that you remind us of your love through our parents. In Jesus' name we pray. Amen.

DAY 2

Q: What is the fifth commandment?
A: Honor your father and your mother.

What does this mean?
Because we love and worship God, we shouldn't ignore or anger our parents, but we should love, honor, obey, and think highly of them.

The longer you live, the more you experience life. If you are ten years old, you probably have experienced going to school, making friends, using money to buy a few things, and learning to swim or ride a bike. If you have a baby sister or brother who is eighteen months old, it's easy to see you know more about life than they do. Makes sense, right? A baby brother or sister has no clue how to ride a bike, go to school, or even tie their own shoes!

So, if your life experience as a ten-year-old gives you more wisdom than a little brother or sister, how do you think that relates to your parents and you?

Here is the thing: Your parents have been your age, but you have not been their age. Sometimes we think we know better than our parents (and when your parents were your age they probably thought they knew better than their parents, too), but it's important to remember that experience in life brings much wisdom. Since your parents know what it's like to be your age, and you don't know what it's like to be their age, it would be wise to listen to their words. This is one of the best ways that you can honor them.

Read *Proverbs 13:1.*

- In what ways do your parents have more experience than you?
- In what ways has your parents' disciplining been a blessing for you?
- Parents, share a story of how you saw the blessing of Proverbs 13:1 in your life when you were young. What wisdom did your parents impart to you? How could you impart this wisdom to your children?

Prayer

Father, please help us to be more wise and see the need to listen to our parents' instruction. As children, may we identify the wisdom of their words, which we don't yet possess, and may we come welcome it more and more as we grow. Help us to grow. Help parents love, serve, and guide to the best of their ability. May we see our need for them and for you, God. In Jesus' name we pray. Amen.

DAY 3

Q: What is the fifth commandment?

A: Honor your father and your mother.

What does this mean?

Because we love and worship God, we shouldn't ignore or anger our parents, but we should love, honor, obey, and think highly of them.

Your parents are not perfect. They know that and you know that. That doesn't mean you don't have to honor them or listen to them: it just means that your parents need to repent of their sins just like everyone else.

One of the ways that families are ripped apart is by not repenting to one another. Repentance is one of the foremost ways that we display that we are truly Christian. In repentance, we show that we are sorry for our sin; we desire to change our ways; we seek trust in Jesus' provision for our sin through his life, death, and resurrection; and by the power of his Spirit, we break our enslavement to that sin.

Your parents need to do this when they sin against you. And one of the ways you can honor your parents is to forgive them for the sins they commit against you. Maybe they raised their voice when they shouldn't have, maybe they ignored you when you needed something, or maybe they disciplined you in unrighteous anger.

If your parents are Christian, they will repent. And God loves it when you honor them through forgiveness. These things sustain a loving bond between you that is hard to break.

Read *Ephesians 6:4.*

- Parents, how do you need to repent to your children? Are there ways you have been exasperating your children? Ask them now.
- Children, why would forgiveness be a way to honor your parents?

DAILY DEVOTIONS

Prayer

Father, thank you that you promise to forgive us when we repent of our sins because of Jesus' life, death, and resurrection. Thank you that Jesus covers us and that you unite us to him. Everything that is true of him is true of us now! May we rejoice in this truth. May we extend forgiveness when we sin against our family. By the power of your Spirit, allow us to know when we need to repent and help us to be willing to do it. In Jesus' name we pray. Amen.

DAY 4

Q: What is the fifth commandment?

A: Honor your father and your mother.

What does this mean?

Because we love and worship God, we shouldn't ignore or anger our parents, but we should love, honor, obey, and think highly of them.

Do you think it's possible to honor someone by ignoring them?

Of course not. What this goes to show is that honoring someone is most often linked to listening to them. When we don't listen to God or our parents, we're communicating that what they say has no value to us.

When someone listens well to you, doesn't that make you feel good? The opposite is also true. When people ignore us, it makes us feel devalued. It's the same way for God and our parents.

Read *James 1:19.*

- In what ways do you need to repent of not listening well?
- Are there ways in which you have not been slow to speak?
- Can you identify a time in your life when you listened well to your parents and it was a blessing to you? *(Parents, if your children can't think of a time, maybe you can help them remember.)*

Prayer

Father, please help us to listen well to our family. May our patterns of speech and action reflect a love to listen. Banish all defensiveness from our hearts because we know that we are secure in you. Help us to listen to you and our parents well. May we honor you as we honor them. In Jesus' name we pray. Amen.

DAY 5

Q: What is the fifth commandment?

A: Honor your father and your mother.

What does this mean?

Because we love and worship God, we shouldn't ignore or anger our parents, but we should love, honor, obey, and think highly of them.

Do you know what a filter is? A filter is something that helps prevent unclean things from going where you don't want them. For example, the heating system in your house has a filter on it so that when warm air blows out, the dirt doesn't get all over your house.

A filter lets good things come through and keeps out bad things out.

Sometimes we need a filter over our mouths. Most conflicts in families come about because of the way we use our words. In fact, one of the most common ways that children dishonor their parents is through their speech. Wouldn't it be nice if we had a filter over our mouths?

God has given us great Bible verses that can serve as a filter over our mouths that, when remembered, can help prevent family conflict.

Read *Ephesians 4:29.*

- What would be one way you could build each other up with your words right now?
- The verse speaks of our needs. Do you know what the needs of your parents are in the way that you talk to them? Parents, do you know what the needs of your children are in the way you talk to them?

Prayer

Father, thank you that you have never uttered an unkind word to us, and in Jesus, we hear your pleasure spoken over us. May we reflect this truth in the way we speak to one another as family. May children love their parents through the honor they show them, and may parents love their children through words of praise, affirmation, and instruction. In Jesus' name we pray. Amen.

WEEK 6

You shall not murder

DAY 1

Q: *What is the sixth commandment?*

A: *You shall not murder.*

Q: *What does this mean?*

A: *Because we love and worship God, we shouldn't hurt or harm other people, but instead we should help them like a friend would.*

Do you know what an image is? Can you describe it in your own words? An image is a visual representation of something—like a photograph. If you were to take a picture of your house, the picture would be an "image" of your house. You can look at the picture and know what your house is like. You can't see all of it, but you can get a good idea of what it's about.

God says that we are made in his image. Human beings are different from all of God's other creatures because he says that we are a picture of him. Because of that, we are more valuable to him than all other creation. That doesn't mean that the rest of creation has no value—it does. But human beings simply reflect God's image the most and are therefore his highest creation.

God values us greatly! He took great pleasure in giving us life. Because of this, God commands us not to murder. Human life is precious to him, and we don't have the right to take it since it's not ours to take. We don't own it. God is the owner of all life since he is the giver of life. We can't take matters into our own hands.

Read *Genesis 1:26–28.*

- Whose image are we created in?
- How does this text show us that we are the highest form of God's creation?
- Why would God want us to be fruitful and multiply?
- How does all this connect with God's command to not murder?

DAILY DEVOTIONS

Prayer

Father, thank you that you have given us the gift of life—a life that reflects you. It is an honor and a privilege to reflect you. May we honor you by cherishing that fact and recognizing the value in others. In Jesus' name we pray. Amen.

DAY 2

Q: What is the sixth commandment?

A: You shall not murder.

Q: What does this mean?

A: Because we love and worship God, we shouldn't hurt or harm other people, but instead we should help them like a friend would.

Sadly, murder happens all the time in our world. It creates a horrible sense of loss for people who love the victim while the perpetrator usually ends up living in fear of being caught, or is caught and must spend the rest of his life in prison.

People who murder usually are people who feel they can't get what they want. They will do anything to get it. Some people love drugs. It's what they want. If they have to murder to get drugs, they will. Some people love power. It's what they want. If they have to murder to gain or maintain power, they will. Some people want respect. They demand it. If they can't get that respect, they will murder those whom they feel deeply disrespected by.

Murder happens because we don't trust God. If we want something, God wants us to ask him, not try to control the situation and feel like we have to do whatever it takes to get what we want. God will provide. Do you believe that? If you really believe that, then we don't have to murder to get what we want.

Read James 4:1–3. (Note to parents: Some of these questions are more "heart-level" questions which your kids may not be emotionally mature enough to engage with. But there is much value in answering them for yourself in front of them and teaching them how to think through it.)

- What causes fights and quarrels among us?
- Are there desires in your life that feel a bit out of control because you are not getting what you think you want, need, or demand?

- How could asking God to intervene shape how you feel about those things you want?
- Most people don't feel the desire to murder to get what they want, but they might be tempted to sin against people in other ways if something stands in the way of their wants, needs, or demands. How do we need to repent of this in our lives? What do you want? *(Maybe your boss at work is disrespectful of you, so you gossip about him/her. Maybe you don't have enough money right now so you are tempted to be impatient with you kids because of stress, etc.)*

Prayer

Father, may your wants be our wants. Help us align our desires with yours so that we can trust you, not ourselves. We want to love our neighbor as ourselves. Keep us from hurting others when we think they're getting in the way of what we want. You are our true provider. We thank you for that. In Jesus' name we pray. Amen.

DAY 3

Q: *What is the sixth commandment?*

A: You shall not murder.

Q: *What does this mean?*

A: Because we love and worship God, we shouldn't hurt or harm other people, but instead we should help them like a friend would.

What if someone were to sneak up behind you with a water balloon and throw it at you, or spray some shaving cream in your hand while you were asleep, causing you to get it all over your face? That prankster may need to prepare himself for some revenge!

Do you know what revenge is? It's what we call "getting someone back." When it comes to practical joking, revenge can be a fun thing, but when it comes to matters more serious, revenge can be a very bad thing.

Revenge is a huge problem that plagues many communities around the world today. If someone murders another out of anger, sometimes family and friends of the victim want to "get back" at the murderer by murdering him. Can you see how revenge creates a vicious cycle? The cycle never stops.

God has a better solution.

DAILY DEVOTIONS

Read *Romans 12:17–21.*

- How are we to treat those who mistreat us?
- Why do we not need to "take matters into our own hands"? Does God care about justice?
- How are we to overcome evil?

Prayer

Father, help us to trust you when we feel wronged. Give us the power to love our enemies like you loved us when we were your enemies. Father, forgive our enemies, because they don't know what they are doing. Would you save them and cause them to repent of their sin? In Jesus' name we pray. Amen.

DAY 4

Q: *What is the sixth commandment?*

A: You shall not murder.

Q: *What does this mean?*

A: Because we love and worship God, we shouldn't hurt or harm other people, but instead we should help them like a friend would.

Did you know that some of God's people have committed murder? The story of the Bible is a story of redemption, and God's loving hand of redemption can even reach out to murderers.

Consider these examples:

- Moses saw someone abusing one of his people, and in anger killed that man.
- King David desired to have another man's wife as his own. He abused his power and arranged to have that woman's husband killed.
- The Apostle Paul, before becoming a Christian, used to participate in the killing of Christians.

All of these men suffered for their decision to break this commandment. Anytime we choose to go against God's will, we choose to seek a painful path not worth taking.

But isn't it comforting to know that God still uses the most unlikely of people for his glory? He can even use someone who does something as grievous as murder.

Read *1 Timothy 1:15.*

- Why do you think Paul thought that he was the chief, or the foremost, of sinners?
- Why did Jesus come into the world?
- If God can save murderers in Jesus, do you think he can save you?

Prayer

Father, thank you that your hand of grace is not far from those who repent of their sin—even of some of the most horrible, like murder. We stand in awe of this amazing grace that is able to truly change us. Help us to extend your radical love to others who need it. In Jesus' name we pray. Amen.

DAY 5

Q: *What is the sixth commandment?*

A: *You shall not murder.*

Q: *What does this mean?*

A: *Because we love and worship God, we shouldn't hurt or harm other people, but instead we should help them like a friend would.*

One day while talking with his closest friends, Jesus began teaching about how God wants us to live as his children. He spoke about many different things, like how to live with unbelievers, how to trust in him when we are needy, how to treat our enemies, and many other amazing things.

He also spoke a word about murderers and said something that was rather shocking: murder is not just physically killing someone but it can even be speaking a hurtful word to another. Jesus broadened the definition of "murder" so that everyone would be guilty and no one would feel more righteous than another.

Read *Matthew 5:21–22.*

- What do you think of these verses?
- If this is the definition of a murderer, then who are murderers?
- When have you said something insulting to someone?
- How can murderers be saved?

Prayer

Father, thank you that you can even save murderers like us. Apart from your grace and mercy, we would all be condemned to hell. Thank you, Jesus! Thank you for rescuing us from our sin! Thank you for life! In Jesus' name we pray. Amen.

WEEK 7

You shall not commit adultery

*(**Note to parents: Due to the graphic nature of the seventh-commandment study, you may want to bypass Days 4 and 5 of these devotionals if the topic of sex is not yet appropriate for your children.**)*

DAY 1

Q: What is the seventh commandment?

A: *You shall not commit adultery.*

Q: What does this mean?

A: *Because we love and worship God, we should lead an innocent and good life in word and action, and we should love and honor our spouse.*

Do you know what marriage is all about? Why did God create marriage? Do men and women get married simply because it sounds like a fun idea to live together for the rest of their lives?

Companionship is a very important part of marriage, but we know that God intends marriage to be a symbol of the loving faithfulness that Jesus has for his people, the church. In this way, marriage is not about us as much as it is about him.

This is why God commands his people to not commit adultery. Adultery is leaving your special relationship with your spouse and trying to have a similar special relationship with another person.

Is this the way that Jesus treats the church? Of course not. He has a passionate love for his people alone: his Spirit never leaves them or forsakes them. We are to model this commitment to one another in our marriages.

Read *Ephesians 5:22–27.*

- How are wives supposed to resemble the church?
- How are husbands supposed to resemble Jesus?
- How does Jesus show his faithfulness to the church?
- Why is committing adultery such a big sin?

DAILY DEVOTIONS

Prayer

Father, thank you that you have given us such an amazing picture of what your love for the church looks like. May you help us show this kind of love in our marriages. May your faithfulness be our faithfulness. Teach husbands to lay down their lives for their wives like Jesus. Teach wives to joyfully submit to their husband's loving leadership. In Jesus' name we pray. Amen.

DAY 2

Q: *What is the seventh commandment?*

A: You shall not commit adultery.

Q: *What does this mean?*

A: Because we love and worship God, we should lead an innocent and good life in word and action, and we should love and honor our spouse.

When a man and a woman get married, they become one. What does that mean? It means that while they are still two distinct persons, they have been so closely united that God views them, in a sense, as one person. They are joined together legally, financially, emotionally, physically, and spiritually.

A married couple doesn't have two different bank accounts: they have one.

A married couple doesn't have different last names: they have one.

A married couple doesn't have any secrets: they know each other in the deepest possible way.

A married couple doesn't sleep in separate beds: they share the same bed.

A married couple doesn't pray all by themselves: they go to God in prayer together.

These are just some examples of how a married couple is united as one.

Can you imagine how hurtful it would be if a wife decided to share money with a man not her husband? Or if a husband shared his deepest secrets with a woman not his wife? You can probably imagine how hurtful this would be, right?

Imagine taking a T-shirt and ripping it down the middle in the front and back. Would you want to wear it? Of course not. It's meant to be one piece of clothing, not two. This is why God commands his people not to commit adultery. It creates problems in marriage that are very hard to undo. You shouldn't take something that is designed to be united together and rip it apart.

Read *Mark 10:6–9.*

- Who originally created marriage?
- Based on this text, why should a husband and wife stay together?

Prayer

Father, may our marriages display a faithfulness to one another that models your faithfulness toward us. Give us the strength to fight sin when we are tempted to not act this way in our marriages. In Jesus' name we pray. Amen.

DAY 3

Q: *What is the seventh commandment?*

A: You shall not commit adultery.

Q: *What does this mean?*

A: Because we love and worship God, we should lead an innocent and good life in word and action, and we should love and honor our spouse.

Have you ever been to a wedding ceremony? If so, what do you remember? Music, flowers, beautiful clothing, lots of photographs, and gifts?

These are all great things that come with a wedding ceremony. But what do you think is the ultimate purpose of a wedding ceremony?

Its purpose is for a man and a woman to stand before God and all their family and friends, and publicly commit to being faithful to each other for life. The married couple enters into what is called a "covenant." Remember what that is? A covenant is a commitment of promise between two parties that is based on a loving relationship.

One of the horrible things about adultery is that it betrays all of the promises that were made on the wedding day. If you commit adultery, you make yourself into a liar.

Satan is the father of lies. He loves it when we lie. The reason he loves it is because lying destroys relationships that God has created to be amazing, especially the marriage relationship. Adultery makes us into liars. And that's why God wants us to remain true to the covenant we've made with our spouse.

Read *John 8:2–11.*

- How does Jesus treat the woman who had committed adultery?

DAILY DEVOTIONS

- Does Jesus say that her sin is no big deal?
- How can adulterers be forgiven?

Prayer

Father, apart from your forgiveness, we would be hopelessly lost. Help us to be true to your word, but when we fail, remind us of your life, death, and resurrection, which gives us new life. Show us that we don't have to live as slaves to sin but rather we can be filled with joy by following you. Protect us from the enemy who loves to make liars out of all of us. Fill us with your Spirit, and keep us near you. In Jesus' name we pray. Amen.

DAY 4

Q: What is the seventh commandment?

A: You shall not commit adultery.

Q: What does this mean?

A: Because we love and worship God, we should lead an innocent and good life in word and action, and we should love and honor our spouse.

Do you have a fireplace in your home? If not, perhaps you've seen one. The boundaries of the fireplace allow safety and freedom to feel the fire's heat.

What would happen if you started a fire in the middle of your kitchen? You could burn the whole house down! Why is a fire in the fireplace good and one in the middle of the kitchen bad?

It's because the fireplace provides the proper boundaries for the fire to flourish. The middle of the kitchen lacks brick walls, a chimney for the smoke, and glass doors to repel sparks.

God has created sex to be like a fire in a fireplace: it was made to stay within the boundaries of marriage between husband and wife for life. If you try and take sex out of its proper boundaries, you run the risk of dealing with a whole lot of destruction.

God tells us not to deviate from this commandment. He loves us too much to let us make a mess of our lives.

Read *Genesis 2:21–25.*

- Who is the author of the marriage of Adam and Eve?
- What boundaries did God create in this text?

- How do we know that God approved of their relationship?

Prayer

Father, sexual sin is all around us, outside and inside the church. You have promised to give your Holy Spirit to those who trust and follow you. We thank you that you have given us boundaries to protect things as precious as marriage. May you fill us with your Holy Spirit so that we would do what pleases you: stay sexually pure for marriage. In Jesus' name we pray. Amen.

DAY 5

Q: What is the seventh commandment?

A: You shall not commit adultery.

Q: What does this mean?

A: Because we love and worship God, we should lead an innocent and good life in word and action, and we should love and honor our spouse.

God has created sex to be a beautiful thing. It is the way for a husband and wife to bond with each other in a way they wouldn't bond with anybody else. This kind of physical closeness should only be shared with a spouse. It is a way of saying to your spouse, "I am yours and you are mine. I am willing to give to you completely, my body included."

Can you see why the ultimate act of betrayal would be to have sex with someone other than your spouse? Can you see why that would be so hurtful?

In the truest sense of the word, sex between a husband and wife is holy. It is not for use in any other kind of human relationship. It is set apart for marriage only.

In the Old Testament, God's people were unfaithful to him over and over again. They tried to have a special relationship with him and with lots of other "gods" (which we know were fake) all at the same time.

But God remained faithful to his people. His mercy triumphed over their unfaithfulness. God wants his people to model his faithfulness with each other in marriage.

Read *1 Thessalonians 4:3–8.*

- What is God's will for us? *(v. 3)*
- Do you see how Paul uses language of family in these verses? How should

DAILY DEVOTIONS

that affect how we think about sexual sin? *(v. 5, If someone is not our spouse, they are our family member.)*

- If we ignore this command and sin against our brothers and sisters, who is that ultimately sinning against? *(v. 8)*

Prayer

Father, we want to be faithful to you and to our spouses in marriage. Help us to make our love for our spouses be based on your love, which never fails. May we show an unbelieving world the beauty of holy love. In Jesus' name we pray. Amen.

WEEK 8

You shall not steal

WEEK 8

DAY 1

Q: *What is the eighth commandment?*
A: *You shall not steal.*

Q: *What does this mean?*
A: *Because we love and worship God, we shouldn't take other people's money or property and cheat them, but instead we should help them improve and protect what belongs to them.*

Where does the desire to steal come from? Have you ever felt the urge to steal something? Do you believe that stealing is wrong? If so, why is it wrong?

Sometimes people steal because they are greedy. Sometimes people steal because they are needy. Sometimes people steal to hurt someone else. In all of these cases, stealing hurts the person being stolen from. And it also hurts the person who does the stealing.

How so? The one doing the stealing believes in a lie, and believing in a lie hurts when the damage is done. God wants us to not steal because it hurts others and ourselves.

Read *Ephesians 4:28.*

- Paul exhorts his audience in Ephesus to stop stealing and start doing what?
- Why does he believe that working hard is important?
- Do you know any people who are in need whom you could bless?

Prayer

Father, help us to not be selfish and greedy. Give us energy to work hard so that we are able to have what we need. May we never dishonor your name in the way we use our money or respond to a lack of money. Help us to trust you instead of resorting to stealing. You have given us ample reasons to believe that you will provide. In Jesus' name we pray. Amen.

DAY 2

Q: *What is the eighth commandment?*
A: *You shall not steal.*

Q: *What does this mean?*
A: *Because we love and worship God, we shouldn't take other people's money or property and cheat them, but instead we should help them improve and protect what belongs to them.*

Most of us wake up in the morning and know that our parents will provide for us, and there is cereal in the pantry for breakfast. But sadly, in some parts of the world, and in some families, food is scarce, or there isn't a parent around to take care of the kids. But if you have a parent reading this to you right now, they are likely caring for your needs and feeding you. You should be thankful for that!

When there is a loving, caring adult around, you don't stress out about whether or not you'll have breakfast in the morning. Similarly, God wants us to remember that he is our heavenly Father and he loves to provide for his children just like your parents love to provide for you. He will be there for you and will give you what you need.

Because this is true, we don't have to steal to get what we need. God will provide what we need. He loves to give good gifts to his children, and he has said that if we have food and clothing, we should be content (1 Tim. 6:8).

Read *Matthew 6:25–33.*

- If you were tempted to steal, do you think these verses might help you stop? How so?
- Why does God command us not to be anxious?
- Do you think God is aware of your needs?
- Can you name some ways that God has provided for you in the past?

Prayer

Father, thank you so much that you have promised to provide. We trust you. The evidence of this is our past. You have been so faithful to give us what we've needed. May remembering this be fuel for our faith. In Jesus' name we pray. Amen.

DAY 3

Q: What is the eighth commandment?

A: You shall not steal.

Q: What does this mean?

A: Because we love and worship God, we shouldn't take other people's money or property and cheat them, but instead we should help them improve and protect what belongs to them.

Do you remember the first of the Ten Commandments? It was that we should have no other gods than the God of the Bible. He alone is the true God over all the universe, and he will have no rivals.

Why do you think God chose to tell us this commandment first? It might be because he knows that we are prone to wander away from him and worship things other than him. He knows that our hearts are like little idol-making factories—idols that we want to bow down to. Can you think of what some of those idols might be in your life that you are tempted to worship?

For many, it's money. If you worship it but you don't have any of it, you might be tempted to steal to get it. If money is our god, then we might feel completely worthless until we get it.

In this way, stealing is really a worship problem. We worship the wrong things. If we can't have them, we hurt other people in order to get it.

But the great news is that God is always ready to give himself to us. He says that he loves to give his Holy Spirit to those who ask him (Luke 11:11–13). He is always near those who humbly trust him. Know that the thing that we need most can never be taken away from us. This perspective helps us battle any desire to steal.

Read Romans 13:9–10.

- How do we fulfill the law?
- Why is stealing unloving?

Prayer

Father, thank you that you are so loving as to command us to worship you and you alone. You know that our hearts are prone to wander from you and worship anything besides you. Our hearts are restless until they rest in you. Draw us near to you as we draw near to you. In Jesus' name we pray. Amen.

DAILY DEVOTIONS

DAY 4

Q: What is the eighth commandment?

A: You shall not steal.

Q: What does this mean?

A: Because we love and worship God, we shouldn't take other people's money or property and cheat them, but instead we should help them improve and protect what belongs to them.

What do you think is the opposite of stealing? If God wants us to *stop* doing something, wouldn't you think he would want us to *start* doing something instead?

If stealing involves taking something that is not ours, wouldn't it mean that the opposite of stealing would be giving something that is ours? What would you call that? The Bible calls that generosity.

Generosity is very important to God because it shows that we understand how he has been so generous with us. Can you think of anything more generous than giving your very life for someone else? That is what God did for us in Jesus. Jesus gave his very life so that we wouldn't have to bear the wrath of God for our sin. The debt was too much, and we didn't have any money. God took our debt upon himself and paid it in full.

Generosity is the opposite of stealing. Our God loves generosity because he is a generous God.

Read *Philippians 2:3–8.*

- How does this text show us Jesus' generosity?
- Can you think of people in your life who have modeled this kind of generosity to you?
- In what ways could you grow in generosity?

Prayer

Father, thank you so much that you have been so generous with us in Jesus. May we have the same mind and heart toward our neighbors and family. May stealing be our last inclination because you have done just the opposite for us. You have given us all that we need that is most important. Thank you so much. In Jesus' name we pray. Amen.

DAY 5

Q: *What is the eighth commandment?*

A: You shall not steal.

Q: *What does this mean?*

A: Because we love and worship God, we shouldn't take other people's money or property and cheat them, but instead we should help them improve and protect what belongs to them.

Imagine a person relaxing on the beach and enjoying a cold drink while the warm ocean air lightly caresses their skin. If there was one word to describe what that person might be feeling, what do you think it would be?

A word that comes to mind is "content." To be content means to be peacefully happy. The Bible says that contentment is something that we should pursue but can only find when we are satisfied in God and the things he has provided.

If we are not made content by God and his provisions, we might be tempted to try and find our contentment in other things and, if necessary, steal to get it. God knows that this will make us miserable in the end, and so that's why he calls us to be content with what we have.

Read *1 Timothy 6:6.*

- What reason does Paul give for why godliness with contentment is great gain?
- How could this verse help us battle a desire to steal?
- Do you feel content with what you have right now? If not, what do you need to be content?

Prayer

Father, we want to be content in you. You have promised that in godliness we will have great gain. May you incline our hearts to pursue gain as you define it and not as our sinful hearts do. Help our unbelief. We know that apart from you there is nothing good or of eternal value. In Jesus' name we pray. Amen.

WEEK 9

You shall not bear false witness against your neighbor

DAY 1

Q: *What is the ninth commandment?*

A: *You shall not bear false witness against your neighbor.*

Q: *What does this mean?*

A: *Because we love and worship God, we shouldn't deceive, betray, or speak badly about other people, but instead we should defend them, speak well of them, and build them up.*

Do you think lying is a big deal? Why or why not?

According to the Bible, lying is a really big deal. It says that Satan is "the father of lies" and that when we lie, we are acting as his children, not God's. Sounds pretty bad, doesn't it?

God commands his people to not lie because it dishonors him and breaks down relationships. How could you have good relationships with God and people if there was constant lying? You couldn't. Everyone would be suspicious of one another and constantly be on edge.

This is the essence of what it means to bear false witness. Since God always tells the truth, he wants his children to be like him, always telling the truth.

Read John 8:44.

- What are some ways Satan has shown himself to be the father of lies in the Bible? *(Garden of Eden, tempting Jesus with lies in the wilderness, etc.)*
- In what ways have you lied?

Prayer

Father, thank you that you have given us the truth and that the truth sets us free. May we live in light of it so that we don't find ourselves in a prison of lies. Thank you for showing us a better way. Help us to truly love others so that we never lie to them. In Jesus' name we pray. Amen.

DAILY DEVOTIONS

DAY 2

Q: What is the ninth commandment?

A: You shall not bear false witness against your neighbor.

Q: What does this mean?

A: Because we love and worship God, we shouldn't deceive, betray, or speak badly about other people, but instead we should defend them, speak well of them, and build them up.

Do you know what the legal system is? It is our system of government here in the United States that tries to get people to follow the laws of the land. If people break them, the system makes sure that they have to pay for their crime.

The system can get very complicated and involve many people. But in biblical times, things were relatively simpler. In those days, what was most important were witnesses. These are people who saw the crime take place. They would be expected to tell the truth about what they saw. If two or three people were united about what they saw, then a judge would usually bring down punishment on the convicted. Sometimes the punishment was very serious, like the death penalty.

Witnesses were key. In light of this, can you see why it would be important to follow this commandment?

***Read** Proverbs 25:18.*

- Why would the author of this proverb use such strong language?
- How would you feel if you were accused of doing something you didn't do and had to bear the penalty for it?
- Does this remind you of the gospel? How so?

Prayer

Father, thank you that you sent Jesus to bear the punishment we liars deserve. He had accusers bear false witness against him and, as a result, bore our punishment. This is amazing grace, to say the least. Because we esteem your grace, may we never lie and thereby hurt someone or cause them to be unjustly punished. In Jesus' name we pray. Amen.

DAY 3

Q: What is the ninth commandment?

A: You shall not bear false witness against your neighbor.

Q: What does this mean?

A: Because we love and worship God, we shouldn't deceive, betray, or speak badly about other people, but instead we should defend them, speak well of them, and build them up.

"Did you hear what she did?" "Do you know where they were last night?!"

Have you ever been in a conversation that started like this? Did it pique your interest?

Usually when someone starts a conversation like this, they are about to do what is called "gossip." Gossip is telling a story about someone that may or may not be true. People gossip either because they feel bad about themselves and fear you might find out things about them that they wouldn't want shared, so they divert attention away from themselves to someone else, or because they want to intentionally cause harm to someone's reputation.

Gossip usually contains partial truths, or lies, that are harmful to the person being talked about. It also tears communities apart. When you gossip about someone, the person listening to you gossip might have a new perspective on that person. For example, if I were talking with you about another person at school whom you had never met and I said, "Hey! Did you know that so and so comes from a poor family, and I heard that they used to live on the street! Isn't that crazy?! I wonder if they are kind of smelly?" As a result of this conversation, you might have a perspective about that person before you even had the chance to meet them. You might think things about them that were not true.

Would you like to be treated that way? Of course not. Gossip hurts people and grieves the heart of God. It's a form of bearing false witness.

Read *Proverbs 18:8.*

- Why do you think the author of the proverb says that gossip tastes so good?
- Can true facts ever be used as gossip?
- Why does gossip hurt people?
- What should you do if someone approaches you with a story that is simply gossip?

Prayer

Father, help us to use our words to love and serve people and not to spread lies about them. May the communities that bear your name resemble you in the way that we speak. Bring life to our conversations so that they may be a blessing to all those who hear. In Jesus' name we pray. Amen.

DAY 4

Q: What is the ninth commandment?

A: You shall not bear false witness against your neighbor.

Q: What does this mean?

A: Because we love and worship God, we shouldn't deceive, betray, or speak badly about other people, but instead we should defend them, speak well of them, and build them up.

Did you know that God exists in community? What does that mean? It means that God is a Trinity. He is the Father, Son, and Holy Spirit. God in three persons. Not three different Gods but three persons, each fully God, who make up one God. It's hard to understand, but by faith we believe what the Bible teaches.

What is important to understand is that each member of the Trinity has a selfless love for the other persons of the Trinity. Their relationship is like that of a husband and wife, who are two distinct persons but yet are one, and the beauty of their relationship is seen in how they love and serve each other. Out of the overflow of this love, they can love and serve their children well.

Do you think the Son ever lies to the Father or that the Holy Spirit speaks falsehoods to the Son? No way! Because they're one, they would never want to do anything to hurt one another. Would it be good for a husband to lie to his wife? Never! They too are as one and would never want to hurt the other.

As the church, God says we are supposed to act the same way. Since we Christians are a church family, we should put away falsehood and seek the health of our community. If we can't take God's call to speak the truth to one another seriously, how can we love and serve those who don't know Jesus? How can we call people to come join us in following Jesus if we're lying to each other?

Read Ephesians 4:25.

- Why does Paul want us to put away falsehood?

- What does being members of one another have to do with lying?
- God calls us to live as a loving community. How does lying destroy that?

Prayer

Father, help us to remember who we are as members of your community, the church. May we love each other well as family. Keep our mouths pure with words of life, and keep us away from falsehood that tear away at our community. We love your church. Thank you for promising to build it. May we build it up as well in the way we speak. In Jesus' name we pray. Amen.

DAY 5

Q: What is the ninth commandment?

A: You shall not bear false witness against your neighbor.

Q: What does this mean?

A: Because we love and worship God, we shouldn't deceive, betray, or speak badly about other people, but instead we should defend them, speak well of them, and build them up.

If God hates lying, what would be the opposite of that? Speaking the truth! God loves the truth. In fact, Jesus said that he *is* the truth (John 14:6).

Sometimes it's hard to speak the truth, especially when you need to say something to someone that might not be fun to hear.

We all need correction: children need correction from their parents; husbands and wives need correction from each other; and Christians need correction for the sake of healthy community. These kinds of corrections are called "rebuke."

If we are going to do that, we have to be willing to speak the truth in love. Sometimes it's easier to just keep quiet or say something that is a bit more comfortable so that the person to whom you are speaking doesn't get his/her feelings hurt. But we still need to communicate the truth, albeit sensitively and gently, if we are going to grow in the ways God wants. We also should be able to receive the truth from others when they speak it to us!

Read *Ephesians 4:15, 16.*

- Why does Paul say that we should speak the truth in love?
- How have your parents spoken the truth in love to you?

DAILY DEVOTIONS

- Sometimes it's hard to receive truth, but wouldn't you say that this has been a blessing in your life? *(Parents might need to do a little coaching here.)*

Prayer

Father, may we be humble enough to give and receive the truth in a way that honors you and helps us grow. Help us overcome our temptation to refrain from truth-telling or to tell a falsehood because we fear the opinions of other people. May we only fear you. In Jesus' name we pray. Amen.

WEEK 10

You shall not covet

DAY 1

*Q: **What is the tenth commandment?***

A: You shall not covet your neighbor's house, your neighbor's wife, or anything that is his.

*Q: **What does this mean?***

A: Because we love and worship God, we shouldn't desire to have the things that belong to other people, but instead we should help them protect what is theirs.

Have you ever wanted something really bad that was not yours? What was it?

This is what it means to covet. It means having a really strong desire for something that is not yours. Why do you think this would be a problem?

One of the reasons this is a problem is that is shows a heart that is unthankful for what you have received from God. God loves to give good gifts to his children, and when we are more focused on what others have than on what we've been given, it says that we think he is a bit stingy.

How would you feel if you gave someone a gift and right after you gave it to them, they immediately started talking about how they wish they had gotten something else? That wouldn't make you feel very good, would it? It would show how unthankful they were, wouldn't it?

Let's honor God by focusing on the blessings he's given us.

Read *James 1:17.*

- Where do all good gifts come from?
- What are some good and perfect gifts that you have received?
- How could you thank God for these?

Prayer

Father, we want to honor you by recognizing that you have given us all we need. Help us to be content and thankful. We deserved hell, and you gave your Son for us. May we first and foremost be thankful for this. Everything beyond is a bonus! Allow our hearts to see things this way. We need your help. In Jesus' name we pray. Amen.

DAILY DEVOTIONS

DAY 2

Q: What is the tenth commandment?

A: You shall not covet your neighbor's house, your neighbor's wife, or anything that is his.

Q: What does this mean?

A: Because we love and worship God, we shouldn't desire to have the things that belong to other people, but instead we should help them protect what is theirs.

Human beings love to compare things: How high can you jump? How fast can you run? How strong are you? These are things boys usually like to talk about when they're little.

We love to compare. This is the heart of coveting or envy.

As we get older we might be tempted to compare other things: *They have such a good marriage! Wow, I can't believe how much money she makes. It's way more than me! She has such beautiful hair. I wish I had that. Look at his car! My car is rusty and falling apart.*

We love to compare. Why do you think God wouldn't want to us to be consumed with comparison?

One of the reasons might be because he wants us to take our eyes off of things that are not eternal and fixate on things that are. Many of the things that other people have that we might be tempted to covet are things that will pass away with time.

Beauty fades. Money never lasts. Cars break down. And houses fall apart. But God wants us to be consumed with him because he is eternal.

Read Luke 12:13–21.

- Did the rich man have his heart set on things of this world or things that are eternal?
- Can you relate to the rich man? Do you think he was envious?

Prayer

Father, may we stop constantly comparing the things that you have given us with the things you have given others. Help us to be content in you. May our vision of you be so grand that the things of this world pale in comparison. In Jesus' name we pray. Amen.

DAY 3

Q: What is the tenth commandment?

A: You shall not covet your neighbor's house, your neighbor's wife, or anything that is his.

Q: What does this mean?

A: Because we love and worship God, we shouldn't desire to have the things that belong to other people, but instead we should help them protect what is theirs.

Imagine your best friend's birthday is around the corner, and you've come up with a gift idea that she would really love. You thought and thought about it and finally have decided on what to get her.

The day of the party arrives, and you give her your gift. She seems to appreciate it but very soon after opening it, she says, "Thanks for the gift, but I honestly deserved something better than this."

How would that make you feel? Understandably, that would probably make you feel pretty bad and maybe a bit angry, right?

What would be a good term to describe your friend's attitude? The Bible calls it "pride"—thinking so highly of yourself that you feel you deserve more than what you get.

This is how we treat God when we covet. Just like how we would feel dishonored if our friend said those words to us, we dishonor God when we fixate on what others have instead of what God has graciously given to us.

Read *Proverbs 16:18.*

- What happens when we are prideful?
- Are there ways you have been prideful by thinking that you deserve better than what you have?
- How do you think we can fight pride together?

Prayer

Father, you have been so good to us. May we not think more highly of ourselves than we should. Rather, help us to focus on how good you are and how we can be loving to our neighbors. Help us not to covet their things. In Jesus' name we pray. Amen.

DAILY DEVOTIONS

DAY 4

Q: What is the tenth commandment?

A: You shall not covet your neighbor's house, your neighbor's wife, or anything that is his.

Q: What does this mean?

A: Because we love and worship God, we shouldn't desire to have the things that belong to other people, but instead we should help them protect what is theirs.

I wish I was like her. I wish I could do what he does. I wish my house was like theirs. I wish my wife was like his wife.

Do these statements sound like they come from someone who is at peace? They don't, do they? They sound like they come from someone who is quite unsettled, in fact.

Coveting causes us to be anxious and uneasy. It robs us of the peace that God wants for us because we are constantly looking elsewhere for fulfillment. A restful heart would say with ease, "God, I am so thankful for what you have given me. It is enough for me."

In today's culture, too many of us are wrapped up in envy and covetousness. We want something so bad that we'll work long hours to earn enough money for it. The problem is that once we get it, we find something else to covet, and we get to work on getting that. See how this causes our life to be a never-ending cycle of futility?

This is not the peaceful and restful state that God wants his children to be in. Envy always makes us miserable in the end.

Read *1 Timothy 6:9, 10.*

- What is it that ruins people?
- How is the love of money closely related to covetousness?
- What are some things that you are tempted to covet?

Prayer

Father, we want to peacefully rest in your provision. Banish from our hearts any love of money, and help us to be thankful for what we have. We don't want to work ourselves to death in pursuit of what does not satisfy. Only you satisfy. Forgive us when we fail to see this. In Jesus' name we pray. Amen.

DAY 5

Q: What is the tenth commandment?

A: You shall not covet your neighbor's house, your neighbor's wife, or anything that is his.

Q: What does this mean?

A: Because we love and worship God, we shouldn't desire to have the things that belong to other people, but instead we should help them protect what is theirs.

Coveting is all about our desires. But are all desires wrong? Can you think of some desires that are good?

Here are some: The desire to satisfy hunger is good. If we didn't try to satisfy hunger, we would eventually die. The desire to have a roof over your head is good. No one wants to be homeless. The desire to wear clothes is good. Who wants to run around naked?!

There are lots of desires that are good, but above them all, God wants us to desire him. He wants us to find our greatest satisfaction in him and him alone. Doesn't it make sense that we should desire the greatest thing in the universe? What is greater than God?! And he is greatly glorified when we do.

Coveting is like choosing to eat a nasty, moldy cheeseburger that you found in the garbage over a really tasty, fancy dinner of all our favorite foods. God doesn't want us to settle for things that don't last and are less than the best. God is the best! Let's only settle for him!

Read *Psalm 73:24–26.*

- According to the psalmist, can anyone take God away from him?
- How do you think you could increase your desire for God?
- In what ways is God way better than all the things we are tempted to covet?

Prayer

Father, thank you that you have given yourself to us. May you be our greatest desire in all the world. We know that our desires are often misplaced and sinful. Forgive us when we fail, and may your glory be what consumes us. In Jesus' name we pray. Amen.

SMALL GROUP STUDY

IMAGINE WHAT IT was like on Mount Sinai as Moses was being given the Ten Commandments: Thunder peels. Flashes of lighting. The trumpet blasting. And the Israelites cowering in their tents, unable to look up at the sky, for fear of God's wrath.

But if this snapshot of the narrative is all we see, we'll miss that God is a loving father who enters into history to reveal his loving will for his people. Context is key. In fact, from the time the Israelites were brought up from slavery in Egypt to when they were given the Ten Commandments, God's love remained resolute: he set his people free to live free—to love God and neighbor. His purpose remains the same for his people even today: he sends us his Son Jesus to release us from sin's captivity and to empower us to live according to his will through his Spirit.

Each Sunday at church and during the week in small groups, we'll hear from God's word and learn how the Ten Commandments can best guide our day-to-day lives. We'll answer four questions as they relate to *image, community, worship,* and *mission.* As we study together, we'll see that the Ten Commandments are not archaic prescriptions for an ancient people, obsolete and without relevance. Their immense practical value will be made clear as they teach us how to live free in light of God's love for us.

SMALL GROUP QUESTIONS

To help focus your group time, it's recommended to discuss each commandment in light of the four following questions:

Image
- How does this commandment impact how you see God, yourself, and others?

Community

- How does this commandment impact your relationships at home, work, and church?

Worship

- How does this commandment impact how you praise God and reflect his glory?

Mission

- How does this commandment impact the bold proclamation of Jesus' conquering Satan, sin, and death?

Please join the Community Groups coaching site, Mars Hill Church's online community, for a weekly coaching video that will help guide you on how to address specific issues and answer questions provided by Pastor Mark's sermons. We hope its timely information will help you lead your group well: http://marshill.com/communitygroupcoaching.

Groups looking to supplement their time with additional application questions also have the option of using the weekly questions provided in the next section of this guide.

WEEK 1

Exodus 20:1–3

"And God spoke all these words, saying,

'I am the LORD your God, who brought you out of the land of Egypt, out of the house of slavery. You shall have no other gods before me.'"

This first and primary commandment is the foundation for all the commandments to follow. God reminds his people who he is and what he has done for them in Exodus 20:2, and then commands his people to put him first, above all else. God is the same yesterday, today, and tomorrow. And as our knowledge of God's character increases, so does our desire to love and worship him above all else. Our knowledge of and intimacy with God is increased through familiarity with his word and time spent in conversation with him through prayer.

Questions

- What characteristics of God's nature are most difficult for you to grasp?
- What characteristics of God's nature are most exciting to you?
- What things do you worship with your time, money, love, or attention above God? How might you worship God first with these things?
- Does your small group put God first in its conversations, time, and practices?

Prayer

Lord God, we thank you for revealing yourself to us in your word. Please send your Spirit to guide us as we seek to worship you rightly. Give us an unquenchable thirst to know you more intimately and deeply. Help us to see how we've loved other people or things above you. We pray that nothing would be more delightful to us than spending time with you. Help us to become a group that values knowing you above all and encourages others to know you better. You alone are worthy of our worship! We praise you and thank you for the guidelines you have given us in your word. Amen.

WEEK 2

Exodus 20:4–6

"You shall not make for yourself a carved image, or any likeness of anything that is in heaven above, or that is in the earth beneath, or that is in the water under the earth. You shall not bow down to them or serve them, for I the LORD your God am a jealous God, visiting the iniquity of the fathers on the children to the third and the fourth generation of those who hate me, but showing steadfast love to thousands of those who love me and keep my commandments."

The second commandment adds to the first and expands on it. God has already told his people to worship him first and foremost, and now he clarifies that this precludes worship of both idols created by man as well as anything created by God. God's steadfast love for his children is seen not only in his jealousy for their ultimate good but also in his love for the repentant.

Questions

- What are some examples of man-made images that are worshiped in our society?
- What idols are you personally most tempted to worship above God?
- God is jealous for our hearts. How are you jealous for the hearts of those you are in relationship with to be worshiping God first? How could you grow in this area?
- This passage addresses "the iniquity of the fathers on the children." This speaks to the consequences of sin. How have the sins of your forbears affected you?
- What changes is the Holy Spirit challenging you to make so that your family legacy is one that speaks of the "steadfast love" of God?

Prayer

Holy God, we are grateful for the steadfast love that gives you a jealous heart for your people. Please grant us the same jealous hearts so that through right worship of you as our God we will encourage those around us to worship rightly as well. Reveal to us the ways we stubbornly cling to our sinful idolatry, and cause us to see it as the contempt for you that it is. Help us to be people who seek to establish with you a new legacy in our homes and hearts. Amen.

WEEK 3

Exodus 20:7

"You shall not take the name of the LORD your God in vain, for the LORD will not hold him guiltless who takes his name in vain."

This commandment forbids the irreverent or disrespectful use of God's name. Whether we use his name casually as a swear word or speak of him in a way that does not acknowledge his greatness and goodness, we are not honoring and worshiping him the way he deserves to be. This reveals an attitude of the heart that is not seeing God and man rightly.

Questions

- How have you maligned the name of God with your speech or actions?
- How could you honor God and still love others well when you hear someone else use God's name irreverently?
- What does it say about our hearts when we misuse God's name?
- Names are important in the Bible. They often have significant meaning to God; he changes people's names to better reflect their character. How does your usage of God's name reflect his character?

Prayer

Father, we want to honor you in all our speech and actions. Help us to be brave and bold when others speak disrespectfully about you. Give us loving words of truth to speak in those moments. Make us aware of what is in our hearts and on our tongues, and help us to be faithful to repent quickly when we are irreverent. Mold us into a people known for great respect of who you are and what you have done. Amen.

WEEK 4

Exodus 20:8–11

"Remember the Sabbath day, to keep it holy. Six days you shall labor, and do all your work, but the seventh day is a Sabbath to the LORD your God. On it you shall not do any work, you, or your son, or your daughter, your male servant, or your female servant, or your livestock, or the sojourner who is within your gates. For in six days the LORD made heaven and earth, the sea, and all that is in them, and rested on the seventh day. Therefore the LORD blessed the Sabbath day and made it holy."

The commandment to keep the Sabbath as a holy day of rest looks very different today than it might have to the ancient Israelites who first received it. Yet the principle of resting from work was established by God at creation and is to be continued by God's people as an act of worship. It is a time to be refreshed and renewed as we reflect on the God who brought us out of our own individual slaveries through the saving, redeeming work of Jesus. This leads us to thankful worship!

Questions

- How have you struggled with "resting?" What does "rest" mean to you?
- What are some ways you'd like to try to incorporate more Sabbath time into your schedule?
- For Christians, the finished work of Jesus is what provides ultimate rest. In what practical ways can you lay down your efforts, striving, and work and rest in the perfect, finished work of Christ?
- How does your group practice Sabbath? How might you incorporate more Sabbath into your group's rhythm?

Prayer

God, we want to worship you rightly with our time. We repent of the ways we have allowed our busy schedules to dictate our lives at times. We ask that you would help us to worship you first by giving you the best of ourselves and our time. Help us to be obedient when we are called to rest in you. Thank you that Jesus has paid it all so we can truly rest in his finished work. Amen.

WEEK 5

Exodus 20:12

"Honor your father and your mother, that your days may be long in the land that the Lord your God is giving you."

Whether we grew up in loving Christian homes, were left to raise ourselves as our parents pursued their own idolatry, or experienced something in between, this week's commandment tells us to honor our parents. This may look very different depending on our circumstances. What is constant is that we have been called by a loving, perfect Father to honor roles he created and intended for good, despite the sin that often mars such a good creation. We therefore honor our parents for God's sake, not our own and not our parents'. We do this based on who he is, not based on who our parents may or may not have been. So, we can all obey this commandment joyfully, because he is *good*!

Questions

- What examples of honoring one's parents have encouraged you most?
- What makes it most difficult for you to honor your parents? How will you worship God by doing this well?
- If your parents are actively sinning against you, in what ways can you still honor them?
- If you are a parent, how can you encourage your children to do this in a way that causes your children to worship God and not you?
- How can you cultivate an atmosphere of honor toward elders in general in your home, group, and church?

Prayer

Jesus, you are our ultimate example of honor toward our parents. Thank you for obeying our Father and going to the cross for us. Remind us every day that you are good, and because you are good we can honor fearlessly. Help us to create climates of honor in our behavior and hearts so that we can encourage children in our lives to honor freely and well. We repent of disobedience in not honoring when we should have. Give us hearts that desire to worship you by honoring others above ourselves. Amen.

WEEK 6

Exodus 20:13

"You shall not murder."

When we look upon another human being, we are not merely looking upon a physical form created by God, but we are looking at the reflection of God that is imaged in that person. This commandment addresses the literal taking of human life, but it also reveals the heart God wants his people to have for others. We are not only to keep from murder, but we are to refrain from behaviors and attitudes that diminish or demean life.

Questions

- Are there certain types of people or people groups that you have a harder time seeing as a reflection of God's image? Why? Is this sin?
- What are some ways that society diminishes or demeans others that is considered socially acceptable?
- Is there someone specific whom you have not honored as a creation of the holy God? How will you repent to that person and begin to honor them rightly?
- When you are demeaning another in your mind and heart, what other emotions are you most often feeling? What does this reveal about what you believe that is not true? Where is your worship landing?
- What could your group do to honor the life God has created in a practical way?

Prayer

Father of the living, we as your creations thank you for the life you have given us. Forgive us for not honoring all you have created as we should. Give us wisdom and direction as we seek to worship you by loving our fellow human beings as reflections of you. When we demean and diminish others, we are demeaning and diminishing you. Help us to love well without any other aim than to worship and please you. Amen.

WEEK 7

Exodus 20:14

"You shall not commit adultery."

The principle behind this commandment is that God desires his people to be free from sexual sin. Every type of sexual immorality, including the sins of the heart, mind, and body, fall into this category. Not only are we to be a people free of sexual sin, we should be actively pursuing sexual purity at all times. Everything about our sexuality should stand as an act of worship—and praise God it can!

Questions

Leaders: We encourage you to separate men and women for the discussion portion this week.

- How are you tempted to sin sexually? How can you turn this temptation into an act of worship?
- What areas of sexual temptation are you minimizing by not recognizing them as sin?
- How can you encourage others to be sexually pure? How would you like to be encouraged in this area?
- Have you struggled with discontentment in your sexuality? How could this become worship?
- God obviously places a high priority on sexual purity—it is a good thing he created, and he doesn't want it defiled. If we don't see sex as a good and pure thing in marriage, we aren't seeing it as God does. How has your view of sexuality not been worshipful?

Prayer

Thank you, Lord, for the gift of our sexuality. We desire to use this gift in a way that honors you. Help us to see sex purely and rightly so that we may worship you in our sexuality. Keep us from the deceit of sin in this area. Do not allow us to become seduced by lies about what is pure and what isn't. May your Spirit help us to be ever watchful, and guard our hearts, minds, and bodies. Amen.

WEEK 8

Exodus 20:15

"You shall not steal."

Stealing is taking something that doesn't belong to you. You may not have stolen anything from a store without paying, but that doesn't mean you aren't, at times, thieves. Stealing is more common than we'd like to think. We steal from others and from God. If God has told you to spend time with your spouse and you choose to have some alone time doing a fun activity, you are robbing your spouse. If you spend your tithe money on a latte and rationalize that it's only a couple of dollars less, at least you're giving something, then you are stealing from God. There are many ways we can have the heart of a thief.

Questions

- When we decide we need something we don't have and are willing to get it at a cost, we are not trusting God to provide what we need. When is it hardest for you to trust that God will provide what you need?
- When there is something you want more than to obey God, how do you rationalize what you do to get it? How has this cost you?
- How do you "steal" in your relationships? Is there something you are avoiding by this theft? Or gaining? How will you repent of this?
- God wants his people to have generous hearts. With what, whom, or when is it harder for you to practice generosity?
- How well does your group practice generosity? How could you grow in this?

Prayer

Father God, give us generous hearts that do not count the gain or the loss in service to you. Help us to worship with our time, relationships, hearts, and money without seeking for gain hidden along the way. Keep our eyes on you, Lord, the one who is unendingly generous from a vast treasure trove. Help our hearts to be content and peaceful, remembering your generosity to those you love and your great wisdom in knowing our true needs. Amen.

WEEK 9

Exodus 20:16

"You shall not bear false witness against your neighbor."

God himself *is* truth and he cannot tolerate any trace of untruth in his people. We need never be afraid to speak the truth because he who is truth stands ready in the gap to uphold us and defend us with his righteous right hand. We live as representatives of Christ, and so all our words and actions must be truthful.

Questions

- When are you most likely to lie? Why is it hardest to be truthful then?
- Have you used this command to speak the truth as a weapon and sinned by speaking the truth less than lovingly? How will you repent of this?
- How else have you been tempted by dishonesty outside of lying with your mouth?
- How have you been hurt by lies? How has God comforted you in this?

Prayer

Truthful Savior, we are deceitful liars, every one of us. We lie with our mouths, with our hearts, and with our actions. Fill us with your truth and help us to speak and live truthfully. Let us be known for our honesty and integrity. Give us courage when it is needed. We belong to you; help us to live as you live, speaking truthfully always. Remind us of who you are when we are fearful and tempted to lie. Thank you that you are always honest, always speak the truth in love, and always convict us when we don't. Amen.

WEEK 10

Exodus 20:17

"You shall not covet your neighbor's house; you shall not covet your neighbor's wife, or his male servant, or his female servant, or his ox, or his donkey, or anything that is your neighbor's."

Covetousness is bred in a heart that is discontent and does not agree with God about what is best and ought to be given you. It is bred in a heart that is prideful and arrogant. In this final commandment, the sins of the heart that cause one to deny God bring us back to the first commandment: to have no other gods before the holy, living God. In our pride, we deny God—who he is and what he has done—because we are not satisfied with our lives, and this breeds covetousness. We can only be truly satisfied and see God rightly when we are not prideful but humble. Humility is the antidote to covetousness. With humility comes contentment.

Questions

- In what areas of your life are you most discontent? Most prideful? Is there any correlation?
- If you could change one thing about your life now, what would it be?
- How does one grow in humility?
- When have you been most content? Why do you think that was?
- What thing, desire, or relationship is God asking you to lay at his feet in humble worship?

Prayer

Glorious Father, we humble ourselves before you. We confess our greed, our covetousness, our discontent, and our pride. We ask for your forgiveness. Grow us up into a people full of humility, contented in you and you alone. Help us to be at peace, knowing that you are sovereign and have our ultimate good at heart. We love you. Amen.

GROUP
INDUCTIVE
STUDY

WEEK 1

Exodus 20:2–3

"I am the LORD your God, who brought you out of the land of Egypt, out of the house of slavery. You shall have no other gods before me."

INTRODUCTION

In a culture awash with do-it-yourself spirituality, diversity is in, rules are out, and to make an exclusive religious claim is to be unloving. In such a culture, telling the average person on the street that there is only one God and that there are rules for life is like spraying a cat with water—it is not received well.

Moreover, pop culture references to God are becoming increasingly more ambiguous. There is no talk of the God of the Bible. Instead, there is a sort of cosmic entity out there called "the universe" or "love." In this context, the Ten Commandments are viewed as merely moral laws—primitive, judgmental, and irrelevant at best.

What this mindset misses is this: guardrails are not antithetical to love, but rather they help promote an environment where love and freedom can flourish.

This is what God intended all along. In giving his people the Ten Commandments, he lovingly reminded them that he was the Lord their God, who brought them out of the land of Egypt, out of the house of slavery. The first commandment thus reflects both God's perfect character and his love. The commandments as a whole are a gift to his beloved in order to show them that life works best in right relationship to God and to neighbor.

"You shall have no other gods before me" is given first because, as the church reformer Martin Luther said in his *Treatise on Good Works*, "This Commandment is the very first, highest and best, from which all the others proceed." In other words, when God's people are enamored with the one true God, the one who saves, all aspects of life are affected, leaving every other object of worship exposed as false and unable to save. The creator knows what's best for his people.

OBSERVATION

***Read** 1 Corinthians 10:5–14.*

The Israelites experienced God's miraculous deliverance, and they enjoyed his lavish love time and again. Yet they did not love, worship, or prefer him to other gods as they had been commanded to. The Israelites serve as an example for us of the danger and destruction that results from worshiping other gods and straying from the safe-guard embedded in the first commandment.

- According to verses 7–10, why did God let the first generation of Israelites die in the wilderness without having reached the Promised Land? (See Num. 14:22–29.)
- What idols did they worship before God? What were the consequences? (See Num. 25:1–9.)
- What will happen if one does not recognize his/her idolatry?

INTERPRETATION

In 1 Corinthians, the Israelites' example is a warning to the believers in Corinth to flee from idolatry, indicating that worshiping other gods is a general human tendency.

- What made their desires evil?
- What do these harsh punishments for idolatry reveal?
- What do grumbling and complaining stem from?

APPLICATION

In this passage we see that listening to God's word is of utmost importance in the life of the believer. In the 1 Corinthians passage, we see an extreme example of what happens when God's people fail to listen to and abide by his word. Just like the Israelites, we too experience the struggle of not listening to God's words of instruction.

Read *Matthew 22:37.*

- When you're not busy with daily tasks (e.g., work, chores at home, commuting), what do you think most about? What is your imagination captured by?
- When was the last time you were truly happy, angry, or sad?
- What do your answers reveal about what your heart is devoted to?

God's laws are good, perfect, righteous and holy. God is so committed to our good that anything other than living in right relationship to him and keeping his commandments is utter death. When we prayerfully ponder this commandment, we all inevitably realize things in our lives to confess. But know that, as 1 John 1:9 says, "If we confess our sins, he is faithful and just to forgive us our sins and to cleanse us from all unrighteousness." When we are honest about our sin of placing other people or things before him, as this verse says, God is faithful to cleanse and forgive us so we can walk away free to worship as he has intended.

WEEK 2

Exodus 20:4–6

"You shall not make for yourself a carved image, or any likeness of anything that is in heaven above, or that is in the earth beneath, or that is in the water under the earth. You shall not bow down to them or serve them, for I the LORD your God am a jealous God, visiting the iniquity of the fathers on the children to the third and the fourth generation of those who hate me, but showing steadfast love to thousands of those who love me and keep my commandments."

INTRODUCTION

Some four hundred years before the commandments were given to Moses, Joseph welcomed the Israelites into Egypt to escape famine. After many generations of living as slaves under Egyptian rule and custom, they were acculturated to the worship of many gods.

God sent Moses to deliver his people out of this environment and lead them to the Promised Land. In Exodus 32, we find them waiting in their camp for Moses to return from Mount Sinai. Their hearts become increasingly unsettled during the wait, and they decide to craft a god of their own. Keep in mind, this was almost immediately after one of the greatest examples of God's mercy and deliverance ever recorded and as he was faithfully providing sweet water and manna to sustain them.

Yet, their hearts still grumbled. They didn't trust him to provide for their needs. God himself was just not enough in their eyes, and they wanted something other than the freedom God had provided.

Though this is an ancient text, not much has changed. We still seek comfort in things created, instead of Creator God.

OBSERVATION

Read *Exodus 32:1–14.*

- As Moses was on Mount Sinai for forty days receiving the Ten Commandments from God, what did the people ask Aaron to do, and what was their reasoning?

GROUP INDUCTIVE STUDY

- Compare God's response to idol-making in these verses to the original commandment in Exodus 20:4–6. What differences do you see?
- Moses implores God to restrain his wrath for Israel's abandonment of their promise. How does Moses react when he descends the mountain and sees with his own eyes what they have done?

INTERPRETATION

Some seven hundred years later, the prophet Isaiah writes of how the children of Israel again forget the infinite greatness of God and his desire to work for their good.

Read *Isaiah 40:12–26.*

- List the specific abilities of God noted in this text.
- What does this teach us about the great, infinite reach of God?
- How does this compare to any crafted idol?
- Why is God so specific with us about his eternal power?
- How does the description of God's character in these verses discourage the idea of trusting in any created thing?

In Romans 1, Paul describes how God has given every man the evidence of himself through what he has created.

Read *Romans 1:18–25.*

- What truths do we learn about God in verses 18–20?
- To whom does Paul say these truths are revealed?
- What choices are made in verses 21–23?
- What idols are exchanged for the glory of God?
- What was the lie that they exchanged for the truth?

We have hope. God's commands are for us, not against us, and they show us his deep, enduring love and desire for us to live in freedom, to worship him alone. He knows that we are going to sin against him and against others. He gave his own Son to pay the penalty for our disobedience; Jesus bore the wrath for our sin on the cross once and for all. His last words were "It is finished."

APPLICATION

- Has there ever been a time in your life when you thought God was not good?

- How in the past have you taken matters into your own hands?
- Which people or things did you most seek comfort in?
- In what areas are you not satisfied? In light of your answer, how can you trust God in the unknowns of life going forward?

If you are a believer and follower of Jesus Christ, saved by his grace, you are given an opportunity to confess your worship of lesser gods. Because of his ransoming blood, our wayward hearts are redeemed so that we may stand spotless before the throne of God.

FOR FURTHER STUDY

"The Expulsive Power of a New Affection" - Thomas Chalmers
http://www.monergism.com/Chalmers,%20Thomas%20–%20The%20
Exlpulsive%20Power%20of%20a%20New%20Af.pdf

WEEK 3

Exodus 20:7

"You shall not take the name of the LORD your God in vain, for the LORD will not hold him guiltless who takes his name in vain."

INTRODUCTION

It is not uncommon in our culture to hear God's name spoken regularly. On television shows, in songs played on the radio, and in our day-to-day interactions, we often hear his name used flippantly to convey awe, irritation, and even a curse. As Christians, many of us flinch when we hear friends, neighbors, or coworkers using God's name in this way. Why does this bother us? And is this what it means to "take the Lord's name in vain"?

God cares a great deal about his reputation. Verbalizing his name in the ways mentioned above is one way of misusing it. But we do this in other ways as well: making false or glib claims about him or his word, abusing the authority he has given us as his children, not speaking truth about God or giving him the reverence he deserves through our words and actions, etc. In doing these, we mar the truth and give others a wrong and often unfavorable view of God. We misrepresent the character of the God who created us, pursued us, died for us, and invites us into his family. These are greater implications than most of us think about when reading this commandment.

OBSERVATION

Read *Deuteronomy 18:20, Leviticus 24:10–17, and Matthew 7:21–23.*

- What are the specific ways God's name is used in vain in these verses?
- How seriously does God take misusing his name? What are the consequences he has set for those who do?
- According to these verses, who is expected to keep this command?

INTERPRETATION

Speaking untruthfully or flippantly about God is a form of using his name in vain, but it is only the beginning. We have the power to malign how others see him by claiming his name and acting in a way that is inconsistent with his character and his work in our lives.

GROUP INDUCTIVE STUDY

- In addition to the ways mentioned above, how else do we misuse the name of the Lord through our words? Our actions?
- What are the implications of God's name being misrepresented? What happens when false statements about God and his character are heard and believed?
- Why does God care so much about the protection of his reputation? (See Acts 4:7–12.)
- In light of this commandment, why is it so important to know God intimately, learning as much as we can about his character and ways?

APPLICATION

It's easy to read these passages and think of "those people" who are guilty of misusing God's name. Maybe you've been a member of a church where the pastor used God's word to manipulate his congregation. Perhaps a friend has justified her habitual sin by telling you that God told her it was his will for her. While we often see this happen in big and obvious ways in and around us, we need to humbly search our own hearts for the ways that we are offenders.

- What are some ways that you have not protected the reputation of God in word and deed?
- Have you seen the consequences of someone getting a wrong impression of God's character? What happened?
- According to the verses above, we should be put to death for misusing God's name and maligning his character. Exodus 20:7 is very clear that we will not be held "guiltless." If you are in Christ, what does this mean for you? (See Rom. 3:23–26 and 10:1–4.) How does Christ's work on your behalf enable you to obey this commandment?
- Through this great love of Christ, we have the ability to not only obey this command by not taking his name in vain, but also honoring him with our words. Read Romans 10:5–13. What does this section say about the positive effects our words about God can have on us?
- Continue in the passage and read Romans 10:14–17. In what ways does honoring God by speaking the truth about him have an effect on others?

FOR FURTHER REFLECTION

Ask God to bring to mind anyone who may have been given a wrong impression of God's character through your words and/or actions. Putting Romans 10 into action, knowing that you are not defined by this (remember, "Christ is the end of the law for righteousness to everyone who believes"), how can you help correct the misconceptions and share with them the grace which you have been given?

WEEK 4

Exodus 20:8

"Remember the Sabbath day, to keep it holy."

INTRODUCTION

The Sabbath rebels against slavery. It opposes tyrant rule and endless labor. We see this in the book of Exodus, where God's chosen people are bound as slaves in Egypt and set free by his power. Subsequently, they are led to Mount Sinai where the law and the Ten Commandments are given to them by God to provide boundaries and guidelines for life in community with him and with one another.

Why are these rules considered good news? It was after wandering in the desert, desperate for clarity and direction, that the law was given to God's people. It showed them what it meant to belong to and follow him. This is why the Sabbath commandment was particularly important for God's people: they were no longer slaves but free to worship their creator God in rest. It wasn't a burden but a blessing.

Now the believer's Sabbath is found in Jesus, the lord of the Sabbath. We can now rest from trying to earn salvation because Jesus has finished his redemptive work on the cross on our behalf (Matt. 11:28–30; Rom. 4:5; Col. 2:16–17). By setting aside a day, we are showing that we are a people who are set apart for Jesus.

OBSERVATION

- Imagine the feeling of being set free as a slave in Egypt. What would have been some of the sights, sounds, and emotions?
- According to Exodus 20:8–10, to whom does the Sabbath apply?
- To cease from work for a whole day would have had implications for agriculture, business, etc. What would those be?

INTERPRETATION

- What description is used in reference to the Sabbath? Why is this significant?
- Observing the Sabbath is not simply a suggestion for how to live a better life; it's a clear imperative from God. Why do you think this is so important?
- What are the consequences for rejecting this command?

GROUP INDUCTIVE STUDY

- What is the parallel between the creation story and the creation of the Sabbath?
- Read Matthew 12:1–8. Why do the Pharisees challenge Jesus about the Sabbath? What does it mean that "the Son of Man is lord of the Sabbath"?

APPLICATION

In our culture, busyness serves to fill a void. When life is filled to the brim, every hour booked, we feel in demand and somehow more worthy. Busyness creates a way to earn status and reassure value, and can reflect a belief that God isn't enough.

And yet, God's command to rest in Jesus' work confronts the idols hidden behind such belief. The idol of self-sufficiency cannot fulfill you; it will never be enough. God's call is to not only rest physically but to rest in deep relationship with him.

- Do you feel at rest in times of Bible study, praise, or prayer? Why or why not?
- In looking at your own life, what is it that makes it hard to slow down and spend time with God?
- It is not a sin to work hard. There are seasons in life that have a heightened demand for us to work harder both physically and emotionally. However, God's command for us to rest in him is not conditional. Where do you turn in moments of exhaustion or fatigue?
- Read Jesus' words in Matthew 11:28–30. What does Jesus offer, and what does he ask of us?
- What does rest look like in your relationships (e.g., with spouse, family, friendships, etc.)? What happens when Sabbath is not practiced?
- What are some rhythms that you could set up to practice Sabbath in your life? What does this look like weekly? Quarterly? Annually? Discuss some ways that you could incorporate intentional rest in your life and that of your family.

WEEK 5

Exodus 20:12

"Honor your father and your mother, that your days may be long in the land that the LORD your God is giving you."

INTRODUCTION

Parents are one of the strongest influences in a person's life—for good or for ill. It is no wonder that they can occupy the place of God in children's hearts—whether seeking their approval or pushing them away in bitterness and pain. Children are privy to their parents' sins, bearing their scars for a lifetime. They may either idolize their parents, allowing their influence to become an identity, or demonize them, based on a history of sorrow and hurt. Or, as is common in Western culture, they may selfishly dismiss the important contributions parents make, minimizing even their role in bringing children into the world.

The Ten Commandments, summed up by Jesus in Matthew 22:37–40, speak of loving God with all our heart and loving our neighbors as ourselves. Our parents are our first "neighbors," and we cannot say we love our neighbor if we do not honor our parents.

God commands all to honor their parents in the fifth commandment. What is honor, and how does one obey this command, knowing that parents and those in authority aren't perfect?

OBSERVATION

Read *Colossians 3:18–4:1.*

- This passage encourages submission to authorities in different contexts. What are they?
- What is the motivation for children to honor their parents?
- How is the slave-master relationship, mentioned in 3:22–4:1, similar to the fifth commandment in their ultimate goal?

INTERPRETATION

Honor, as it pertains to honoring those in authority, comes from the Hebrew word *kabbad*, which means to be weighty or heavy. Honor is to treat others with respect, regardless of whether or not they deserve it, understanding the weight their position demands. The opposite of honor in Hebrew is *nabil*, which means to make light of or to curse.

Let's examine how Jesus carried out the "weight" of this command.

- Jesus honored his Father in heaven. In his darkest hour, what was his response to the Father's will? (See Lk. 22:41–42.) How did Jesus seek to please the Father?
- How did Jesus honor his earthly parents? (See Lk. 2:41–52.) Why did he do it?
- In Philippians 2:5–11, we see that Jesus, though fully God, lived a life of humility. What is humility, and how does it relate to honoring God and others?

APPLICATION

Jesus lived a perfect life of obedience and honor. He fulfilled the ultimate requirement of the Ten Commandments in our place, and he incurred God's wrath for our failure to do so. Because Jesus took our sins of dishonor, selfishness, and pride upon himself (2 Cor. 5:21), we are now free to walk in grace, understanding our new identity, or who we are apart from our earthly parents, as those deeply loved by our Father in heaven.

In Christ, we are entrusting ourselves to the most trustworthy authority in the universe. With Christ, by the power of the Holy Spirit, we can learn to honor our parents, loving our first neighbors as ourselves. Through Christ, we can honor our parents, not so that God will love us and approve of us—he already does—but because we are free to love and forgive them as he has loved and forgiven us. And because of Christ, our lives are testimonies of his faithfulness, of turning darkness into light and rescuing his own from the power of Satan to God. We are now living in the gospel, lavished with grace.

- As sinners, honoring and obeying is inevitably difficult. It is even more so if you believe it is devoid of purpose. What is the truth about the Father's hand in your life? Amid any pain, what helps you to trust that God is good and will work all things for good as he has promised (Rom. 8:28)? What keeps you from having that trust?
- The gospel of Jesus enables parents to love their children well and to live worthy of their child's honor. When have you seen the gospel change the way you respond to your children? What are some things we can do to

allow the gospel to penetrate deeper and let it improve the way we treat them?

- How does honoring imperfect parents reflect the love God has for us? If your parents were absent or have sinned grievously against you, how does God say he will meet you? (See Ps. 68:5; 27:10.) When have you seen the body of Christ help meet that need?

Take some time this week to seek the Holy Spirit for his leading in your relationship with your parent(s), remembering that, above all, our lives are lived for the glory of God. What would give him the most glory in your response to your parent(s)? Do you need to forgive, repenting of anger and bitterness? How should you express your gratitude to them for their sacrifice? Do you need to pray for them? Do you need to seek counseling for the wrongs they've done which you've haven't been able to face? By the power of the Holy Spirit, Jesus will work in and through you as you submit your will to the will of your Father in heaven.

WEEK 6

Exodus 20:13

"You shall not murder."

INTRODUCTION

Joseph had led his family to Egypt in the safety and protection of the Pharaoh. Years later, however, the new king of Egypt mandated that all midwives would, upon seeing the birth of a Hebrew son, kill him. When the midwives refused to comply, he commanded, "'Every son that is born to the Hebrews you shall cast into the Nile'" (Exod. 1:22). God spared Moses from this fate, and he also saved his people's lives through Moses as he led them to the Promised Land.

God wants his people to live in freedom. He doesn't just protect our life; he gave us our life when he created us and breathed his breath into us (Gen. 1:27; 2:7; Ps. 139:13–16). Because God treasures life, the sixth commandment "You shall not murder" is not just about what not to do; it also implies what to do—be life-giving to the people around you.

God not only gives us life; he gives us *new* life through redemption. Because of what God has done, we're able to love him and each other, sharing his joy with others through our thoughts, words, and actions.

OBSERVATION

While you may not have physically murdered someone, we are all implicated by this command when we take into context the entirety of Scripture.

- In Matthew 5:21–22, we see Jesus teaching on Exodus 20:13 and explaining how murder is not just the physical act. What do emotions, thoughts, and words reveal about the human heart?
- Read James 4:1–3. What is the root of war and murderous desires? Who are we thinking about when we focus on our passions, desires, and envy?

INTERPRETATION

Because of the richness of God's grace and mercy, we can draw near to him and be filled with his Spirit rather than the murderous intent of our hearts. As God's people, we can be empowered by his Spirit to bless others with life.

- Many of the commandments are summarized in the command to love. Read Romans 13:8–10. How does love overcome murderous intents? How does love put anger at our brother in perspective?
- Who in Luke 10:29–37 shows love, and how does it give life to the man who was robbed?

APPLICATION

- God gave life and embedded his image in each person. What are we doing to God's image and ultimately God himself when we hate another person?
- It's not always sinful to be angry. But consider the last time you experienced anger. Why were you angry? What does the abovementioned passage in James 4:1–3 reveal about your words, facial expressions, gestures, or other actions?
- Why is it dangerous to allow anger, envy, or hatred to fester into bitterness?
- While many of us may never physically kill another, we may tolerate certain political policies that do. What kinds of things do we tolerate from the government or via social norms that the Bible might define as murder? What should our response be?
- Read Proverbs 10:11 and 12:18. What does it mean to give life or healing through your words? Think of an example of when someone's words have blessed you, and share it with the group. Have you ever blessed anyone with life or healing through your words? Who in your life would benefit from your words of kindness, mercy, or healing?
- Rather than inaction or negative action, Christ calls us to love others through our actions. (See Prov. 31:8–9; Ps. 82:3–4; Matt. 25:31–40.) Ask God to give you eyes to see the suffering around you and open your heart to another's heartache. What life-giving action(s) do you need to take?

WEEK 7

Exodus 20:14

"You shall not commit adultery."

INTRODUCTION

One of the most infamous stories in Scripture regards adultery, where a powerful king of Israel, King David, seduces a beautiful woman, Bathsheba, while her husband is away at war (2 Sam. 11). In the opening few lines of text, we learn prior to their adultery, King David was not supposed to be home in his palace but out on the battlefield fighting on behalf of God's kingdom. One evening while out for a walk, King David spots Bathsheba bathing and sends a messenger to inquire about her. The king's servant reminds him that Bathsheba is the wife of Uriah the Hittite, one of his soldiers. Not dissuaded, David summons Bathsheba to his palace where they commit adultery, and she conceives.

Although King David was known to be a man after God's own heart (1 Sam. 13:13–14), at the time that he committed adultery with Bathsheba, God was no longer the object of David's greatest desires. His lusts were. He continued to pursue those lusts by inquiring about her, despite warnings, and looking at her merely as an object to be used to gratify his sinful desires.

We may be tempted to ask ourselves, "What does this commandment have to do with me?" while soothing ourselves with affirmations that at least we haven't committed that sin. But Jesus, at the Sermon on the Mount in Matthew 5:27–28, brought radically new teaching that superseded the Old Testament Law and Prophets for believers by saying, "But I say to you that everyone who looks at a woman with lustful intent has already committed adultery with her in his heart." Sexual sin, including lust, is a grievous affront to God and others, and the penalty is death.

OBSERVATION

Read *Matthew 5:17–20; 27–30.*

- In this context, how familiar would the audience Jesus was teaching have been with Moses' law? How would Jesus' words, effectually saying, "The Old Testament condemns adultery, but I say that lustful thoughts will condemn you to hell just the same," have challenged their beliefs?

- In Matthew 5:19, Jesus tells the crowd, whoever "relaxes," or sets aside, the law and teaches others to do the same will be called the least in the kingdom. What is Jesus communicating about the standard of fulfilling the requirements of the law?
- Matthew 5:28 used the word "already." How does this word reveal one's standing according to the law?
- According to Romans 8:3–5, what is the hope for fulfilling the requirements of the law?

INTERPRETATION

Marriage is a sacred covenant promise that is so significant that God describes it as a reflection of the great mystery of Jesus and his bride, the church, for whom he died (Eph. 5:32). Believers, by grace, are able to experience and give the world a picture of Christ's love and devotion through marriage.

- Christ's commitment to his bride is so exhaustive that he loved us while we were yet unfaithful (Rom. 5:8) and gave up his life that we may live (Eph. 5:25). How does adultery misrepresent Jesus and his covenant with the church?
- Jesus explicitly affirmed that marriage is a continuing, lasting commitment—"What therefore God has joined together, let not man separate" (Matt. 19:6; Mk. 10:9). How does God's definition of marriage differ from that of our culture?
- The Bible defines adultery as lust or sex outside the bounds of a legal and monogamous marriage *(porneia)* and warns us against those who would call evil good (Isa. 5:20). How is God's goodness revealed in his commandment prohibiting adultery?
- God intends oneness in marriage (Gen. 2:24) and love in our relationships (Mk. 12:28–31). What does Philippians 2:1 say is the source of our strength?

APPLICATION

Jesus' sermon is not merely given to display humanity's inability to obey God's laws: it does that, but it also provoke our hearts to cry out to him for mercy. Believers who have been reconciled to God through Christ have constant cause for thanksgiving, as we have been given Christ's perfect righteousness as our redemptive solution and can therefore boldly approach his throne!

- In what ways have you minimized lust in your heart, fantasies in your mind, and technical "lines" you've crossed?
- Thinking back to a time when you found yourself lusting after someone, whether an actual person or a fantasy, what was it that you were craving most?
- How is comparing your spouse to another evidence of not treasuring God?
- What lustful thoughts or adulterous actions do you need to confess to God? To others?
- Read Colossians 1:13–14; 2:13–15. What comfort does the gospel bring in light of these confessions?

FOR FURTHER STUDY

Read Psalm 51, a psalm of repentance, and 2 Samuel 11:1–12:31.

RESOURCES

- Kent Hughes, *Preaching the Word* (Wheaton, Ill.: Crossway Books, 1989), 91–111.
- http://marshill.com/media/doctrine/covenant-god-pursues
- "Staying Married Is Not About Staying in Love," Part 1, http://www.desiringgod.org/resource-library/sermons/ staying-married-is-not-about-staying-in-love-part-1#/listen/excerpt.

WEEK 8

Exodus 20:15

"You shall not steal."

INTRODUCTION

When we have money in our wallets and the ability to purchase what we need for life by the work of our own hands, we may feel that we get a free ride when we hear the Lord say, "You shall not steal."

Yet, in these four compelling words, the Lord has more in mind than bank-robbing avoidance. God's economy holds out a message of true kingdom community, wooing us toward loving our neighbors, specifically as it applies to treasures. Enjoying the generosity of all we have received from Christ, we are compelled not to just ask, "Have I obeyed this commandment?" Instead, we are on a journey of wanting to become increasingly cheerful givers like him.

OBSERVATION

- Who is giving this command? Look up Psalm 24:1 and Job 41:11 to discuss who the Lord is in regard to ownership, what that assumes of the receivers of this command, and why it matters.
- The Lord makes a statement in Exodus 20:2 prior to the commandments. How does this retrospective verse give context to the particular sin of stealing?

INTERPRETATION

Read *Deuteronomy 25:13–16.*

The word "steal" feels far away and easy to judge until it is specific. Make a list out loud together of modern day forms of stealing and greed in business, home ownership, forms of monetary spending, home budgeting, personal spending, church stewardship, and even spiritual gifts and talents. Which descriptions unveil more about the heart of a thief?

GROUP INDUCTIVE STUDY

Read *Luke 12:15–21.*

- How would the character in this passage define the Lord's role in ownership, and how does that line up with Psalm 24:1 and Job 41:11 from earlier? How does his view of God affect behavior and choices?
- At what point in the story does the rich man become a fool? Why?
- What does it mean to be "rich toward God," and what would that look like in this story?
- Discuss "sins of omission" seen in this passage (i.e., not doing what the Holy Spirit has asked you to do).

Read Ephesians 4:28. In this verse, the Apostle Paul has more in mind than sin avoidance. What is the end result of no longer stealing and learning an honest work ethic?

Read the following passages as a group. Discuss what you learn about God and Satan. How do the actions of Christ matter in a discussion on thievery?

- John 10:10–11
- Acts 5:3
- Romans 8:31–32
- Ephesians 5:1

APPLICATION

Near antonyms of "steal" presented in the Merriam-Webster's Dictionary are "buy, purchase; bestow, contribute, donate, give, hand over, present." These words recall the victories and gifts of the gospel and show that Christ's work is the antonym of thievery in our lives. Christ bought our lives. He purchased our pardon. He bestowed us a new identity. He contributes every blessing to our lives. He gives us all we need for life, especially himself. God handed over his son, though it was we who deserved death. He has presented us with full life.

God gives; Satan steals. God is generous with good blessings; Satan has nothing good to give, so he can only take. God is jealous for what is his; Satan is envious for what is not his. Jesus humbled himself and became nothing in order to win every blessing to pour over us richly. In our flesh, we resemble the nature of our enemy, living for ourselves and even taking what we have not been given. In Christ, we are transformed and can imitate his love for our neighbors with lavish generosity.

Read the questions below and then allow a moment for the Holy Spirit to prompt one question most relevant for each participant to answer.

- Do you struggle to "act honestly" in your spending or giving at home, work, or church with credit card debt, generosity, living within your means, or tithing?
- Deuteronomy 25:13 asks the question, "What's in your bag?" Have you been hiding a purchase from your spouse by getting rid of the bag, hiding it in your closet for a time, buying it with cash, or being dishonest by purchasing it in a "superstore" under the disguise of a grocery bill? Did you technically buy something honestly but in your heart you stole it because it was out of your budget, dishonest to your spouse, or birthed from covetousness?
- Acknowledging a sin in your heart is not full confession. Confession is agreeing with God, taking it to the cross of Christ, being broken over it, having gratitude for the gospel of Jesus, confessing verbally, and walking away from it in worship of God as your true treasure. What do you need to confess? Do you fear this? If so, read Ephesians 5:13–14.
- If you are struggling with the desire for possessions, it may be helpful to answer this question: how does God view you as a believer? (See 1 Jn. 2:1 and Eph. 2:4–10, noting the Lord's attitude demonstrated). How could the "immeasurable riches of God's grace" battle your desire for riches, for your good and freedom?

FOR FURTHER STUDY

Listen to John Piper's sermon on Philippians 2 here: http://www.desiringgod.org/resource-library/sermons/the-mind-of-christ-looking-out-for-the-interests-of-others.

WEEK 9

Exodus 20:16

"You shall not bear false witness against your neighbor."

INTRODUCTION

Have you ever been put on the spot and, in fear, told a lie? Maybe you've wanted to save face in front of peers or avoid rejection from your spouse.

Common phrases for bearing false witness include "tell a little white lie," "fudge the numbers," "stretching the truth," or "omitting facts." Whatever we call it, whatever the severity of the lie, to bear false witness is to lie about the God we represent.

Everything Christians do and say should always bear "witness" to the truth. Christians are representatives of Jesus who, at every opportunity, sought to show others the exact representation of the God who is truth (Heb. 1:3; Jn. 14:6). Believers speak the truth with their mouths, and they testify to that truth by living in response to the truth of who God is and what he has done for sinners.

OBSERVATION

- What are some ways Christians commonly bear false witness to the gospel beyond just telling lies with their mouths?
- What other commandments are violated when we "bear false witness"?

INTERPRETATION

- Colossians 3:9–10 is a reminder of the tenth commandment. What additional information here gives fresh hope for believers today?
- Proverbs 6:16–23 tells us that lying is one of the things the Lord hates, and then it goes on to tell us how to safeguard against this sin. How do we do that?
- According to Ephesians 4:15, as believers grow in grace, how are they to speak to one another?
- Read 1 Corinthians 13:4–7. When love is present in the life of a believer, how does it respond to truth?

GROUP INDUCTIVE STUDY

APPLICATION

- In Psalm 5:8–10, the psalmist says that his enemies "flatter with their tongue." Are you ever tempted to be less than truthful to flatter either yourself or someone else? Why? Have you considered that this is sin? How could you respond differently in those situations to remain truthful and loving?
- Jesus told his disciples that they would be set free by the truth (Jn. 8:31–32). Ask the Lord to reveal to you any lies you may believe or lies you have told.
- If you have ever despaired of being able to accurately determine truth from lie, you can praise God. God not only delights in the truth, he is truth. Read Psalm 51:5–7, and make it a prayer of your own.
- Perhaps you have been so hurt by lies that it is hard for you to trust your heavenly Father to be truthful to you always. Read 2 Samuel 22, a song of praise written by David to God after God rescued him. David knew that "The word of the Lord proves true."

WEEK 10

Exodus 20:17

"You shall not covet your neighbor's house; you shall not covet your neighbor's wife, or his male servant, or his female servant, or his ox, or his donkey, or anything that is your neighbor's."

INTRODUCTION

When God frees us, he does two things: he frees us from the oppression of sin and death, and frees us to enjoy relationship with him. While believers are set free, never does freedom mean that we are not dependent on God. Even as we seek to obey the commandments, we are never self-reliant. But sadly, oftentimes in the Christian life, we go it alone and settle for mere external obedience and self-reliance. But God never intends mere external obedience. Instead, he is seeking worship from the heart. The last and tenth commandment shifts the gaze from mere rule following to heart motivations.

The tenth commandment reveals the sin of discontent. At the root of discontent is covetousness, the desire to have what doesn't belong to us. In the midst of our covetousness, may we be satisfied in Jesus alone as the ultimate source of our contentment.

OBSERVATION

- A theme of the Ten Commandments is protection. Commandments 1–4 protect our relationship with God, while commandments 5–9 protect our relationship with others. Who or what does the tenth commandment provide protection for? From whom or what?
- How is this commandment similar to commandments 5–9? How is it different?

INTERPRETATION

- To covet means to "earnestly desire." According to 1 Corinthians 12:31 and 14:1, can earnest desire ever be good? What is the difference between the earnest desire commended by Paul in 1 Corinthians and that in the tenth commandment of Exodus 20?

GROUP INDUCTIVE STUDY

- In the tenth commandment, God not only wants to govern our deeds but our motivations and thoughts. In light of James 1:14–15, why is this necessary?
- How might love of the wrong thing and discontent manifest in your walk with God?
- Read Philippians 4:10–13. In what circumstances of life do you find yourself feeling discontent? What is Paul's secret to contentment?
- Read Romans 7:7–12, 21–25. According to Paul, what is the purpose of the law in our salvation story? Paul is a student of the Jewish law, yet he writes here of his struggle to keep it. How does he describe this "war within him," and how is it resolved?

APPLICATION

- In Luke 12:15, Jesus warned the crowd to "Take care, and be on your guard against all covetousness for one's life does not consist in the abundance of his possessions." What currently consumes your thoughts? How are you influenced by the outward appearance of others' lives?
- Is there anyone you are envious of right now? What about their life or possessions do you want? What do you wish God would give you that you don't currently have?
- In what life circumstances are you discontented? If God's love is the source of contentment, what aspect of it is difficult for you to believe and why?
- In what ways are you content in Jesus and what he's done in your life? How might that inform your desire for a different picture of your life?

APPENDIX
FOR
LEADERS

APPENDIX FOR LEADERS

HOW TO USE THE DAILY DEVOTIONS

The following devotions were written in the hope that families would rally around the word of God, grow in relationship together, and discover the Ten Commandments anew to receive wisdom for life and to recognize, as God's children, our need for him in all aspects of life.

Every day, you and your family are provided with a short devotional passage from each of the Ten Commandments. In order to encourage the memorization of the commandments, each devotion begins with a catechism question and answer adapted from Martin Luther's *Shorter Catechism*.

At the time of the Protestant Reformation, there was a high priority put on catechesis as it encouraged heads of household to take responsibility in teaching their children the faith. And catechisms are in a perfect, easy-to-memorize format that kids love. Read each question aloud and encourage your kids to memorize each of the answers and repeat them back to you. The goal is to commit to memory each commandment and its meaning.

A series of questions and illustrations will help you dig deeper into the passage and apply its message to your lives. Each devotion is capped off with a suggested prayer.

Don't feel bound to follow every step, read each word, discuss all the questions, or pray every prayer. Follow the Holy Spirit's lead and allow the conversation to progress as you see fit.

Also, don't stress if you miss a night or get off track with your conversation. Family time can often be a little chaotic, and things come up. Just be prepared to pick up where you left off. Most families aren't able to do devotions every night of the week, so each Scripture portion is divided into five devotions for five days of the week, allowing you the freedom to figure out what weekly rhythms make sense for you.

HOW TO USE THE SMALL GROUP STUDY

This study has been designed to help your small group discover the timeliness of the Ten Commandments for today and to also "stir up one another to love and good works" (Heb. 10:24). To help focus your group time, it's recommended to discuss each commandment in light of the four following questions:

Image

• How does this commandment impact how you see God, yourself, and others?

Community

• How does this commandment impact your relationships at home, at work, and at church?

Worship

• How does this commandment impact how you praise God and reflect his glory?

Mission

• How does this commandment impact the bold proclamation of Jesus' conquering Satan, sin, and death?

Also, please join the Community Groups coaching site, Mars Hill Church's online community, for a weekly coaching video that will give you tips on how to address specific issues, answer questions derived from Pastor Mark's sermons, and find timely information that will help you lead your group well. Visit http://marshill.com/communitygroupcoaching

Groups looking to supplement their time with additional application questions also have the option of using the weekly introductions and questions.

Each study begins with an introduction that serves as a springboard for conversation in your group. There's no need to read the introduction verbatim if that feels stodgy. Just familiarize yourself with the content beforehand, and give an overview of each commandment.

After setting the stage for the week's commandment, questions are provided so that the group can dive into application. Use these as a way to stir up conversation. Some questions are simply opportunities to share testimonies while others are offered as challenges for growth. Take some time beforehand to jot down notes of what questions are best suited for your specific group, and see where the Holy Spirit leads the conversation.

Last is a suggested prayer. It's common to leave little time for prayer, but be encouraged to provide a good amount of time for this. From petitions for help with life's common struggles to praises about answered prayer and everything in between, we need to be refreshed by God's presence, strength, and courage. Pray with expectation that God will do great things in your community. He is a loving Father who loves to give good gifts to his children.

HOW TO USE THE GROUP INDUCTIVE STUDY

What is an inductive study?

"Inductive study" refers to a particular type of study that uses the Bible as the primary tool for learning about God and receiving instruction about how to live a godly life. Our goals for this type of study are to observe the text, interpret its message as we listen to the Holy Spirit, and apply its meaning to our lives.

The steps are simple. Begin by reading the "Background and Introduction" of the assigned Scripture. Then, read the commandment and the associated passage, and pray about what it is communicating, asking God to open your hearts and minds so that you can learn more about him.

Next, examine the passage in light of the context in which it was written, with an eye toward the whole of Scripture. Then, zero in on the words on the page. Good questions to ask as you study include *who, what, where, when, why,* and *how.* Here are some examples of how you might use these kinds of questions:

- Who was the writer's original audience?
- What issue was being addressed? What was being said?
- Where and when did this take place?
- Why was the message given?
- How was the message communicated?

Other helpful questions are listed under the "Observation" heading.

The "Interpretation" will come from the text that is before us, as guided by the Holy Spirit, who opens our eyes and reveals what we need to see. Again, please pray that God will be guiding your mind as you examine the text. Keep in mind that as we study the Ten Commandments, it's important to follow the text and let it define the context and audience *before* jumping into our own life application. That's where the above-mentioned questions are so helpful. Who were the Israelites as recorded in the book of Exodus? What struggles and hardships did they face? How might their struggles inform how we approach our struggles today?

Next, don't miss the "Application" questions. In the fourth section of the weekly study, questions that focus on application are provided. How do each of the commandments shed light into your life? In what ways do the commandments show you your need for Jesus? What is your plan for change going forward?

Finally, pay attention to how God is stirring and convicting your heart. It's here at this intersection where we apply the word to our lives. We become more like Christ, and our relationship with God is deepened.